BENEDICT
CUMBERBATCH

The publishers would like to thank the following sources for their kind permission to reproduce the pictures in this book.

Plate Section 1

1) Rex Features/ITV, 2) Mirrorpix, 3) Rex Features/ITV, 4) Rex Features/Moviestore Collection, 5) Rex Features/Alastair Muir, 6) Rex Features/c.Focus/Everett, 7) Rex Features/ James Curley, 8) Rex Features/Alastair Muir, 9) & 10) Mirrorpix

Plate Section 2

11) Getty Images/Dave M. Benett, 12) Rex Features/Donald Cooper, 13) Rex Features/c. Touchstone/Everett, 14) Getty Images/Jon Furniss/WireImage, 15) Rex Features/c.Focus/ Everett, 16) Rex Features/Dan Wooler, 17) Rex Features/Paramount Pictures/Everett Collection, 18) Rex Features/c. Touchstone/Everett, 19) Rex Features/Moviestore Collection, 20) Getty Images/Simon James/FilmMagic

Every effort has been made to acknowledge correctly and contact the source and/or copyright holder of each picture and Carlton Books Limited apologises for any unintentional errors or omissions, which will be corrected in future editions of this book.

The source material for Benedict Cumberbatch is located at the back of the book, set out under chapter and appendix headings. If an individual or a publication is quoted without being named in the text, consult the endnotes section for identification.

Published in 2014 by André Deutsch
An imprint of the Carlton Publishing Group
20 Mortimer Street
London W1T 3JW

10 9 8 7 6 5 4 3 2 1

Text © Nigel Goodall 2014
Design © Carlton Books Limted 2014

A CIP catalogue record for this book is available from the British Library.

ISBN 978 0 233 00416 7

Printed and bound by CPI Group (UK) Ltd, Croydon, CR0 4YY

BENEDICT
CUMBERBATCH

NIGEL GOODALL

ANDRE
DEUTSCH

In loving memory of my dear friend Rich Samson

Contents

Introduction

Despite what the tabloids may tell you, the great showbiz myth of the overnight star is just that – a myth! Long before she found her rainbow route to immortality, Judy Garland was plain old Frances Ethel Gumm, touring Depression era America with a vaudeville sister act. Norma Jean Baker could tell you exactly how many casting couches and bit parts it took to create Marilyn Monroe. And Ruby Keeler, frantically tap-dancing on *42nd Street*, could have told you that the line "You're going out there a youngster, but you've got to come back a star" was great for the movies but hardly reflected the struggle needed to get ahead in showbiz.

Nevertheless the concept of the overnight sensation persists and is wheeled out to greet every new actor who has made it big after training long and hard. The latest "overnight star" is Benedict Cumberbatch. As Sherlock Holmes in the BBC's radical contemporary re-working of Conan Doyle's Victorian detective, he was greeted by both the press and public as though he had landed on our TV screens a fully formed acting legend.

He had, of course, achieved the impossible, taking an iconic figure from popular culture and re-inventing him for a new audience without losing any of the original's charm or originality – something his *Frankenstein* stage co-star Jonny Lee Miller had less success with in *Elementary*, an American attempt to pull off the same trick. Overnight, Benedict Cumberbatch was an acting sensation with a massive hit on his hands.

Like all the best overnight stars, though, Benedict Cumberbatch seems to have been preparing all his life for the part that would change his life. He comes from a showbusiness family; his father is the actor Timothy Carlton and his mum is 1970s television favourite Wanda Ventham.

His star quality was spotted at the public school Harrow, where his drama teacher described him as the best schoolboy actor he had ever worked with. Given those early encouraging words, as well as his background, it was perhaps inevitable that he would go on to study drama at university in Manchester. Since 2001, he has been a regular in leading British theatre productions, working with the Royal Court, the Royal National Theatre and the Regent's Park Open Air Theatre, receiving award nominations and plaudits for his work in a wide range of roles.

Sherlock did not premiere on British television until 2010, though, and that's when the storm truly broke – though you wouldn't have had to have been that keen-eyed a viewer to have spotted the now famous profile on TV several years earlier. He was hardly a face in the crowd when he made two appearances in family favourite *Heartbeat* in 2000 and 2004, and from there he went on to appear in shows as varied as *Tipping the Velvet, Fortysomething, Cambridge Spies, Spooks* and *Silent Witness*, a good solid body of work.

In 2004 he was nominated for a BAFTA Best Actor award for his performance as Stephen Hawking in an acclaimed television biography. Then there was *Stuart: A Life Backwards* and even a part as a Miss Marple suspect in *Murder is Easy* to prepare him for the criminal investigations to come at Holmes's Baker Street apartment.

At least now he no longer needs to worry about being hailed an overnight sensation, for Hollywood was soon calling and the parts are now becoming increasingly important and impressive. Yet again, though, it's lazy journalism to suggest that the Cumberbatch effect started to take hold only when *Sherlock* became such an enormous hit.

As far back as 2006 he was playing Pitt the Younger in the slavery drama *Amazing Grace*, landing himself a British Breakthrough Acting Award from the London Film Critics Circle. Subsequent big screen hits included heavyweight dramas *Atonement, The Other Boleyn Girl* and *Creation*. Add *Tinker, Tailor, Soldier, Spy* and Steven Spielberg's *War Horse* to the list – not to mention a voice-over role as Smaug the Dragon in *The Hobbit* – and you have a film CV that can only impress.

Star Trek Into Darkness was probably the one that cemented his position as the latest British actor to become a major Hollywood player. The *New York Daily News* said he delivered one of the best blockbuster villains in recent memory – no easy thing to achieve when you're competing with the latest round of CGI! Added to all that, in November 2013, he was presented with the BAFTA Los Angeles Britannia Award for his "masterful performance in television, film and theatre."

With this sort of acclaim, though, comes the inevitable press interest in his life beyond the camera, and Cumberbatch is not alone in his distrust of press intrusions into his privacy. It's a matter of record that he had a relationship of more than a decade with actress Olivia Poulet. Now he is a single man who enjoys extreme sports, and is also supposed to be a Buddhist.

Perhaps the strangest incident in his life away from the stage and camera was a kidnapping attempt in South Africa in 2004, when he and two friends were held at gunpoint. He has since said of the incident: "It taught me that you come into this world as you leave it, on your own. It's made me want to live a life less ordinary."

All the signs now indicate that a life less ordinary is exactly what Benedict Cumberbatch will achieve as his career continues in the ascendant. But with the promise of so much more to come, now is the ideal time to look back on what has already been achieved.

Chapter 1
Nightmare in Paradise

Benedict Cumberbatch is about to be executed. Kneeling on the ground with a duvet over his head and his hands tied with shoelaces, the actor is now in the classic execution position as he awaits the gunshot that will end his life.

It would take Benedict another five years before he could recount the story of that dreadful night when three gunmen took him hostage. He was 28 years old and had flown to a BBC set in South Africa in the summer of 2004 to shoot the series *To the Ends of the Earth*. It was the first time he had gone overseas to film on location, and it was one of his first major screen roles. Alongside him on the set were *Coronation Street* and *Queer As Folk* actress Denise Black and local actor Theo Landey.

The three of them had bonded from the moment they met, and so it seemed quite natural for them to spend time together, both on and off the set. When they finally got a break in the filming schedule, the three took off for a few days to nearby Sodwana Bay to try out the scuba diving and bars that the local unit crew had been raving about. Benedict, Denise and Theo loved the place when they got there, and without any hesitation, they decided to make a long weekend of it. It would give them the chance to soak up the atmosphere until the very last possible moment before they had to return to the set. They had planned to drive back on the Monday morning, but then they had second thoughts about the timing of their journey. What if they got caught up in the traffic and were late? No, they all agreed, it would be best if they headed back after the sun had set on the Sunday evening. And with Benedict going down with a heavy cold, it seemed like a good idea. Little did they know just how badly their new travel plans would turn out.

Police had warned them against travelling on the roads after dark. Carjackings in the area were on the increase, and with so many guns in circulation, good Samaritans were few and far between if you did get into trouble. If you were held up, the advice was simple: never look robbers in the eye, never answer or fight back, and don't make any sudden moves. Just hand over everything asked for, and then hope and pray for your survival. The police had also warned the friends what to expect in such a situation. The robbers would frisk them for weapons, cash, valuables and drugs, and would likely go through their pockets twice, search any bags in the car, separate cash from bank and credit cards, and then demand PIN numbers for the bank cards. The gunmen would usually take a victim hostage to ensure the cards and PIN numbers worked. They would put the prisoner into the boot of the car, drive to a cash point and then, when they had withdrawn the maximum amount of money, shoot their hostage. One can only imagine the sheer terror that must have been going through Benedict's mind when he was the one bundled into the boot.

To this day, no one knows if the puncture that forced the friends off the road was an accident or deliberate. Either way, the full story of what happened next is extraordinary for its raw and frightening brutality. "It was deeply, deeply scary," Denise said of those first moments when the gang approached them. Little did she realize at that point that it was about to get a lot worse. The first time they were frisked by the gang, they were told to face the car and put their hands on their heads. If they'd had a lot of cash on them, the police say, their ordeal would have ended then – the robbers would have taken it and disappeared. But the friends had used up all their cash paying for a diving course. All they had in their pockets were loose change and bank cards, and that in itself made the gunmen angry.

"They bundled us back into the car and I remember thinking that they wanted to shoot us in the car and then drive it off the road," Benedict recounted years later. However, the gunmen had other ideas. Within moments they were on the move. Denise and Theo were pushed on to the back seat while Benedict was forced on top of one of their captors in the front. His back was squashed against the windscreen, and in a moment that would have been funny if it hadn't been so terrifying, he remembers his backside was bashing into the radio controls as the car bounced over the sandy ground. For a brief, surreal moment, Radiohead's "How To

Disappear Completely" blared out of the car speakers. But no one could. The driver turned it off and all they could hear was the sound of the car engine and the bounce of that one punctured front tyre.

When the short journey was over, the fear intensified. Benedict, Denise and Theo were dragged out and lined up alongside each other. They were made to kneel on the ground with their hands on their heads. Then they had a duvet pulled over their heads to muffle the sound of gunshots. "This is it," Benedict remembers thinking. All three of them were waiting for the end. But it didn't come. Even though the gang had been searching through the car, they couldn't find anything worth taking. They were entirely empty-handed and they didn't like it. That was when they got really angry.

"They tossed the duvet off us and demanded to know who owned the phones and why we had no cash or drugs," continued Benedict. "Then the men changed the car tyre, demanded the PIN numbers for our cards and moved onto the next stage of their ugly, violent process. They ordered me to stand up and get into the boot of the car." He had no choice but to comply with their demands. The boot was dirty, dark and small. The boot lid was slammed shut and through it, he could hear the muffled sound of Denise and Theo pleading for his life. And he started to pray for theirs.

Years later, when she first talked about the incident, Denise said the group's acting skills may have helped them through those vital moments. "We were terribly polite and also we were terribly scared," she recalled. But they could talk and they could improvise.

They could play whatever part their captors wanted them to play. And it seemed to work. Somehow, and she doesn't remember how, she and Theo persuaded the men to open up the car boot.

Benedict took some gulps of air, and then played on the fact that they were English actors and that the police would be looking for them. He claimed he was claustrophobic and could have a heart attack in the boot. "I will be a dead Englishman in your car. Not good," he told them. The gunmen thought about it, but decided they didn't care. The boot was slammed shut for a second time. Benedict was again lost in the darkness, struggling to breathe and convinced that this time his fate was sealed. But unbeknown to the three friends, the nightmare still had plenty of time to run.

Benedict listened to yet another ferocious argument among the gang before the boot was opened again. He was then dragged out onto the roadside away from Denise and Theo, and led up a nearby hill. Falling, he cut his head and then was forced to kneel on the ground again. His hands were tied with the laces the robbers had taken from his own shoes. "Make one mistake and we will kill you," the gang threatened. "Lie on the ground," they demanded. A few moments later, Denise and Theo were dragged up alongside him. The South African night had now grown cold.

The three of them tried to lie close for warmth and comfort. "I could feel the blood on my face and hear the insects scratching around in the dark. I thought of home and how, despite being near other people, we all die utterly alone," Benedict said in the article he wrote years later for The Prince's Trust charity. The various gunmen came and went for some time. Unable to communicate with each other, Benedict, Denise and Theo had no idea what was happening or why. Then, at last, they heard the sound of their car driving away. Was it over? Could they get up?

The three of them gradually dared to hope. They managed to untie each other's hands and stumble back towards the main highway. More than three hours had passed since the nightmare had started. It was now almost midnight. They flagged down every passing vehicle but none of them stopped or even slowed down. They walked on into the night, clutching at each other, tears streaming down their faces. Then, having seen the worst of the world, they experienced the best of society.

Far in the distance they spotted a truck stop. It was a sort of shop and café run by elderly local women. They stumbled into it, and for the first time that night, they felt safe. Benedict remembers the old women's anger at what the three of them had experienced in their country. He remembers an old man helping to untie one of the last laces on his wrist. He recalls the tears. Today, almost a decade later, the pain and the fear of that night have faded, but the memory of it will never go away. Nor will the effect it had on everyone involved. "I'm not wasting my time now," declared Denise in the aftermath of it all. Neither was Theo. Nor Benedict. Experts say you are a different person when you have stared violent death in the face. In some ways you are stronger, you have been tested and you have survived. You carry the experience with you in everything you do. By the end of that terrible South African night, Benedict had been given a second chance at life, and he now wanted to make the most of it, to make every second count.

It reminded him of what he said that April: "Life's very precious. You've got to give it 120 per cent. Just celebrate the fact that we're alive and enjoy it."

However, it would take another five years before Benedict could recount the detail of his ordeal, and it would not be until December 2013 that he would talk about the days following the incident. That's when he told *GQ*'s Stuart McGurk about the morning after, when he had walked out onto the balcony of the house he was staying in and gazed out to sea. "I felt heat on my face and I looked across and thought 'I want to swim in that sea, I want to walk across that dune, I want to be with those people I can see playing. Every atom of me wants to be part of it, because I'm alive.' I went to see a counsellor, who said, 'Maybe write this out, speak to people about it, and do some exercise – be part of your landscape.'"

And that's exactly what Benedict did, or rather what he had already done by the time he spoke with the counsellor. True to his hyper-aware nature, he had written four pages detailing the experience while waiting on the roadside for the police, gone skydiving in the days that followed, returned to work and spoken to everyone about it. "I'd already done the check list, it was just intuitive." After his parents flew over the following week, he even revisited the site. "They said, 'Are you sure you want to?' I said 'yes.' You can't imagine all the small details that came back to me. Right down to the insects."

The only trauma Benedict says he identified occurred a few weeks later, when he resumed filming. They were shooting under the deck of a boat on a covered section of dock. He came up for air and a smoke, only to see that they had started to close the main shutter entrance. "I saw the daylight being blocked out and I said 'Look, can you stop that?' But it kept closing and I was like, 'please keep it open!'" He panicked and ran outside. "I smashed my fist three or four times against the brick wall. It was the anger of being reminded of the fear, and where I'd gone in my imagination. And I remember thinking 'Don't let that be the legacy of this.'"

It was a remarkable attitude for someone who had almost died in the most savage of ways, but then again, Benedict is used to near-death experiences. Since his early years, he has almost died on three separate occasions – not counting the South African episode – and he has survived everything from hypothermia and a bomb explosion to dehydration and near-starvation. Yet when people think of Benedict Cumberbatch, it's likely the only near-death experience that comes to mind is the one that didn't actually happen. And of course that was make-believe for the cameras, when Sherlock leapt from the top of St Bartholomew's hospital and seemingly plummeted to his end.

Chapter 2

A Boy From Hammersmith

Timothy Carlton Cumberbatch and Wanda Ventham would never have been described as conventional parents, and the world in which they circulated was scarcely typical either. They were, after all, actors, who had appeared in almost every popular television programme of the 1970s, the decade in which they had met on the set of *A Family at War* in Ireland and fallen in love. Wanda had already filmed two episodes by the time Tim arrived on the set in April 1970, and it was during her third episode – to be broadcast on ITV later that same year – that she would first share scenes with Tim.

Wanda was born in Brighton, Sussex, and at the time she met Tim was best known for her role as Colonel Virginia Lake in the science-fiction series *UFO*, and for her episodes with Roger Moore in *The Saint*. She had also played Number 8 in Patrick

McGoohan's now cult classic *The Prisoner*, the follow-up series to McGoohan's previous outing as secret agent John Drake in *Danger Man*, which Wanda had also appeared in. In fact, Wanda had appeared in so much over the years, it was easier to keep up with what she hadn't been in.

She had taken roles in everything from *Heartbeat*, *Hetty Wainthropp Investigates* and *The Rag Trade* to Arthur Daley's love interest in *Minder*, Susan's mother in *Coupling*, and Deborah's mother in *Men Behaving Badly*. And, not least, she played the lead role in the 15-part BBC series *The Lotus Eaters* opposite Ian Hendry, made a guest appearance in *Rutland Weekend Television*, and appeared in other comedy shows such as *Executive Stress*, *Next of Kin* and *The Two Ronnies*. She even popped up in *Doctor Who* on three different occasions over three decades. Of course, one of her most popular outings was as Cassandra's mother in *Only Fools and Horses*.

Like Tim, who was equally busy appearing in episodes of *Minder*, *Bergerac*, *The Professionals* and *Dick Barton*, Wanda came from the same acting generation as Judi Dench and Maggie Smith – not that she ever intended to be an actress. She originally held aspirations of becoming an artist and attended art school for one year, working as a scenic painter for the Connaught Theatre in Worthing during her school holidays. It was this, her first exposure to professional theatre, which prompted Wanda to leave art school and pursue a career in acting. However, she was forced to turn down her big break to work at the Royal Shakespeare Company because she had fallen pregnant with her first child by her marriage to businessman James Tabernacle. At the time of meeting Tim, and with a nine-year-old daughter in tow, this marriage was well on its way to a natural end.

Although Tim could hardly be blamed for the marriage breakdown, nonetheless he was exactly what Wanda needed to help her make the final decision to split with Tabernacle for good. It also helped that Tim was a romantic. According to an article in *TV Times* some years later, he would send Wanda a perfect single rose every Monday morning; even when he was away filming or on tour, the rose always arrived. Unfortunately, Wanda's daughter Tracy – then aged 13 – had just reached that vulnerable age when nothing seems worse than watching your parents go though the process of splitting up. However, according to Wanda, Tracy was mature enough to realize her parents didn't have a happy relationship any more, and the girl never took sides.

If anything, Tracy leant towards her mother. "I think that's because she always lived with me," explained Wanda. "That is where her security and her continuity came from." Tracy was still at school when she attended her mother's wedding in April 1976, six years after Wanda had met Tim. At the time, Wanda was heavily pregnant with Benedict. Tracy's only objection, it seemed, was her mother's choice of wedding outfit – jeans, held up by braces. But then again, it was the 1970s, when anything was acceptable.

Probably the last thing Tracy had expected, though, was to gain a baby brother when she was well into her teens. Benedict Timothy Carlton Cumberbatch was born on Wednesday, 19 July 1976, at 12pm, in Hammersmith, west London. Born under the astrological sign of Cancer, Benedict was given his two middle names after his father, and shared his birthday with such other notables as Queen guitarist Brian May, Grammy Award-winning pop singer Vicki Carr, romantic painter and engraver John Martin, inventor Samuel Colt (whose legendary Colt revolver is said to have won the Wild West) and the once number-one tennis player in the world, Ilie Nastase.

If one is looking for a marker in history for the day Benedict arrived in the world, there is little to tie it to, apart from a couple of stories from the world of music – that the Allman Brothers' roadie, Scooter Herring, had been sentenced to 75 years for providing drugs to the band, and that another rock band, Deep Purple, had publicly announced they had disbanded after months of personal turmoil and below-par performances. And totally unrelated to music or anything else that was going on in the world at that time, the Sagarmatha National Park in Nepal opened to the public.

Even five days later, when the *Daily Mirror* ran a story about "Wanda's Little Wonder", there was little in the news to shout about. It is probably why the newspaper, then one of Britain's most popular, published photographer Freddie Reed's picture of Benedict under the headline "Little Big Ben takes a bow." Looking at the picture today, both Tim and Wanda couldn't look happier; she is shown beaming at the camera while he pecks her on the temple; front and centre, is nine-pound Benedict looking more alert than most new babies, calmly gazing back at the camera. It is one of the earliest photos known to exist of young Ben, taken just days after Tim had helped to bring him into the world at the

Queen Charlotte and Chelsea Hospital – to this day, one of the oldest and best- known maternity hospitals in Europe, and at the time of Benedict's birth located at Goldhawk Road, less than a 10-minute drive from where the Carlton's home was located in Kensington.

Although the Cumberbatch name is said to have German and Welsh origins (it supposedly means "a person who dwells in a valley with a stream"), the family heritage and history is decidedly more British. According to family historian Debra Chatfield, the Cumberbatches were a prominent English family of merchants and adventurers in the eighteenth and nineteenth centuries. Abraham Cumberbatch, Benedict's fifth great-grandfather who lived from 1726 until 1785, was from Bristol and founded the family fortunes on a sugar plantation in Barbados. Today Benedict shudders at the knowledge that there appear to be many Cumberbatches whose ancestors were slaves, and took their name from the family that once owned them. In 2006, when Benedict starred in a film about the abolition of slavery, *Amazing Grace*, he described his role – as prime minister William Pitt the Younger – as a "sort of apology" for his ancestors. Not that he needed to apologize for his grandfather, Henry Carlton Cumberbatch, a highly decorated naval commander who had fought in both world wars.

But there was also a much darker side to Benedict's family history, on his mother's side. His great-great-uncle was arrested and charged with stabbing a friend to death in August 1893. The relative, Henry Ventham, was just 14 when he and Frederick Betteridge, another 14-year-old, went blackberry-picking down a country lane near their Hampshire village. The teenagers were said to have had a terrible row, resulting in a fatal knife wound for Frederick, who was found with the blade still lodged in his chest. But Henry pleaded not guilty when placed in the dock at Hampshire Assizes in Winchester. He was dramatically cleared on the evidence of a third boy, who said the tragic lad accidentally ran on to the knife. A jury accepted Henry's claim that the death was unintentional and found him not guilty of both murder and manslaughter. An account of the case was published in the *Hampshire Advertiser* on Saturday, 18 November 1893, which headlined the stabbing case near Romsey, and concluded how "His Lordship was quite content with the view the court had taken of the case."

Just six months after Benedict's birth, his own young life was once again being chronicled in the *Daily Mirror* as the newspaper reported his mother's television and theatrical career. Having been out of the limelight for some time, Wanda had now decided the time was ripe for her to return to acting in the TV series *Crown Court*. The media was naturally eager to find out how Wanda would handle childcare for her baby son. Whereas most parents would be faced with domestic upheaval, for Tim and Wanda, arrangements couldn't have been more straightforward. Tim, who was then working during the day on the television version of *Dick Barton*, would babysit Ben at night while Wanda was treading the boards on stage in the theatre.

Not so good, however, was the night when Benedict first cheated death. Tracy, Benedict's half-sister, was babysitting him in the middle of winter – and she put the crying baby on the roof of the family's Kensington top-floor flat to calm him for a moment or two. It had worked dozens of times before: when Benedict cried, his parents would carry his pram up to the roof so he could gaze up at the sky. He would smile, become still and would often sleep. "But then," laughs Benedict at the memory today, "she forgot about me! It was funny. She was in the kitchen with her friends and she suddenly saw snow falling through the window." When she ran upstairs, she found Benedict serene, teeth chattering but still smiling. He had to be thawed out on a radiator before his parents returned home. "I had literally turned blue."

When Wanda returned to television in a *Doctor Who* episode, it again generated interest from the press, and once more provided an ideal opportunity for Wanda to mention young Benedict in her interviews. It was October 1977, and Tom Baker was the Doctor, a role that, interestingly enough, Benedict himself would one day consider himself for – as the eleventh incarnation, before Matt Smith was cast, and shortly before Benedict won the role of Sherlock. The *Doctor Who* story in which Wanda appeared was titled *The Invisible Enemy*, and was the episode that introduced K-9, the robot dog, to viewers as the Doctor's latest companion. Benedict, who was then just 15 months old, however, wouldn't be able to see his mother on the small screen in the popular science-fiction series. "My one regret about *Doctor Who*," Wanda told journalists, "is that Ben is too young to watch it."

Two years later, when Ben would still have been too young for *Doctor Who*, there was something else to worry about – and that was Benedict's confusion over Father Christmas. According to Wanda, then starring in the popular television drama *Fallen Hero*, it was the first year Benedict really understood about Father Christmas and he was very excited about it. "But he is a bit puzzled because he has been taken by friends to see two separate Father Christmases, and he can't understand why there were two faces! He's worried, too, that Father Christmas will come down our chimney and land on the electric fire."

Even as a three-year-old, it seemed the young Benedict was thinking ahead and already making some curious observations. Wanda's solution was simple. She would remind him that the family would be spending the holiday at his grandmother's in Brighton, where the fire would be extinguished in plenty of time for Father Christmas to visit, and where there would be an old rugby sock on his bed to hold the presents Father Christmas would surely bring.

Certainly, descriptions of Benedict as a child seem to vary widely, depending upon whom is asked. His mother remembers he was a most considerate, sweet boy, but when Peter Stanford caught up with Benedict for a *Daily Telegraph* interview in August 2012, the actor referred to himself as having been a "hyperactive nightmare." Certainly, he confirmed there were times when his mother was less than pleased with his conduct. One of those times was when Wanda was interviewed at home in 1979, and she ended up apologizing for her three-year-old's "vile" behaviour. Although Tim did his best to entertain a "boisterous Benedict" in another room, the article described him as "an energetic handful, who was treating the living room like a sports stadium." But according to Wanda, "his temperament has gone slightly loopy in the last day or so, because he recently had his tonsils removed."

By the following year, it seemed Ben had calmed down to a certain degree. Either that or he was on his best behaviour when around his mother's friends. Una Stubbs, best known as the girl who danced her way through Cliff Richard's *Summer Holiday* and *Wonderful Life*, and a decade later, as Alf Garnett's daughter-in-law in the controversial *Till Death Us Do Part*, had worked on a number of movies with Wanda, and would eventually, years later, work alongside Benedict as *Sherlock*'s Mrs Hudson. She remembers going out in her Kensington neighbourhood with the pram. "Wanda and I would be talking, while poor little Benedict, who I suppose was about four, was standing there while we were gossiping in the high street for hours!"

Such quiet memories, however, were seldom recorded in the press. Often Benedict's life, away from acting, seemed thrilling or daring, but never quiet. Above all else, he seemed fearless as a child and indeed, in later life, American actress Elaine Stritch once predicted that Benedict would be very successful as an actor. But despite the comment, perhaps even she could not have foreseen exactly how successful. "She predicted my future career when I was a little boy," laughs Benedict. "She saw me walking across a field in my red dungarees despite the presence of a bull. 'That boy,' she drawled, 'is going to be a star.'" His ability to charm anything in his path was just one of his remarkable traits, even when he was too young to recognize it.

Even though Wanda probably found being a mum hard work and thoroughly enjoyed her acting career, the one thing she didn't want to miss out on was her son's childhood. As she explained at the time, "Ben starts school next year and because I'd worked for some long spells away from home making *Fallen Hero* last year, I decided to spend as much times as possible with him this year. I turned down any job which involved leaving London for more than a few days." Certainly, the bond between Benedict and his parents appeared to be very close, much the same as it is to this day. They often visit him whenever he is working in theatre or on film and television sets, and if he is working overseas, he frequently mentions them during his interviews.

What is perhaps strange, though, is that being in the public eye for much of his childhood doesn't seem to have deterred Benedict from becoming an actor himself and following his parents into the limelight. Neither does he appear to have outgrown any of the behaviour noted from some descriptions of him as a child. In a BBC Press Office article of May 2005, the writer described how the actor kept cast members in stitches with his impressions of other people, sat nervously on his hands, bounced his leg up and down during interviews and had bouts of uncontrollable giggles. It's as if he is unable to contain his energy. Even an early school report gives much the same impression: "Ben is slightly more controlled, but he must try to be less noisy. A good start, but we hope Ben will calm down a little next term."

If talkative and energetic are the best words to describe Benedict as a child, then it was something his mother confirmed during a radio show interview in 2010. "He always talked a lot, had a very loud voice, was very active, but he always slept. I think he knew he had an older mummy, and he was very kind to me." During the same interview, Benedict agreed, but was also quick to admit, "I'm very grumpy without eight hours sleep, which is a luxury in adult life."

Another luxury, as an older child, was being allowed to accompany his parents on a six-week theatrical tour during a break from school, and watching from the wings of the stage while his mother performed. But, as Wanda remembers, "he got terribly overexcited because of the laughter. And he was standing there, actually shivering, saying 'I wish I could come on with you.'" In a later interview with Gary Oldman for *Interview* magazine, Benedict elaborated: "I went to visit my godmother, who was at Stratford at the time, and she let me stand on the stage. I just remember looking out into the darkness, and it pulled me in, rather than pushed me away, if you know what I mean. It gave me a real energy and thrill to think about communicating with that, rather than turning away and going home and having a cup of tea and leaving it to someone else. And as adults, they just looked at each other with raised eyebrows, all three of them actors, and went, 'Oh dear.'" According to Benedict, it was one of the first moments that he recalls when the pieces of the acting jigsaw started falling into place.

Another part of the jigsaw, some observers suggest, was how quick off the mark Benedict always was when it came to developing his observation skills. As a youngster, one of the actor's most telling attributes was his tendency to study people around him. According to an interview he did with the *Guardian* in July 2010, he recalled how he and his parents "lived sort of in the shadow of the Royal Garden Hotel in Kensington, where there were floors and floors of all these silhouettes, and I was fascinated with people doing things. I was far too young to know what was going on, if indeed anything was going on. But I always listened through the door jamb to this adult world, to see what was going on." And as he became more famous, and easily recognizable on the street, he mourned the loss of such opportunities to observe others unaware. "One of the fears of having too much work is not having time to observe. And once you get recognized, there is nowhere for you to look any more. You can't sit on a night bus and watch it all happen."

Neither could he resist the opportunity to start acting in school plays. Recalling an early role as Joseph in his prep school's nativity play, he gained notoriety by shoving Mary off the stage because he was "furious about how self-indulgent she was being." Unwittingly, he earned a laugh from the audience, but playing to the crowd to get that laugh was not his intention. He simply wanted the performance to go as it should and, even as a youngster, was more focused on the performance than courting audiences or his parents' approval. "Mum and dad were mortified, but I pushed Mary off stage because she was taking too long. Actresses eh!" he joked with Darren Dalglish of the London Theatre website years later.

When Benedict's parents were told he had finally settled in at school, they were thrilled. He had been enrolled at Brambletye School as a boarder when he was just eight years old, and at the time, no one was quite sure if he would cope. The school was set in a stunning location of 140 acres of glorious countryside in

West Sussex and was then, as it is now, a leading day and boarding preparatory school for children from aged two and a half to 13. It was well known for teaching boys and girls in small classes and preparing them for the top senior independent schools in the country, providing an enormous breadth of opportunity in which children could develop their own individual talents within a very supportive network. The dedication and enthusiasm of the staff were very distinct and every child was encouraged to get the most out of school life. It was reportedly an extremely happy school, but was it right for Benedict?

To start with, Benedict reckoned he was a city boy and didn't like leaving London. His parents flat had a roof-top terrace and he used to love going up there to watch helicopters take off and land at Prince Charles and Princess Diana's home in nearby Kensington Palace. But his parents felt he needed the stability that only a school in the country could provide. As actors, they were always on the road, often heading off to distant theatres and film sets for months at time. They worried that the upheavals weren't good for a little boy who couldn't sit still. They weren't the only ones. The very controlled, exceptionally polite and well-behaved Benedict we see today wasn't often in evidence in his childhood or while he was at Brambletye.

All the same, a few years later, he was happy to share the laughs on and off stage when he won a role in his first Shakespeare play at school. He had a lot of fun playing Bottom, one of the comedy characters in *A Midsummer Night's Dream*. He also laughed out loud when he saw his photograph and read his first ever review in the school magazine in which the critic noted that "Benedict Cumberbatch's Bottom will be long remembered."

In many ways, Benedict was still a hyperactive nightmare, and even worse, a tearaway, for most of his time at Brambletye. Few people who knew him in those days could have predicted he would turn into a polished, well-mannered adult. For back then, he got into fights and into trouble on a near daily basis. Ultimately, he says, teachers pushed him towards both sport and the stage as a last-ditch attempt for some desperately needed behaviour management. At three, that bad behaviour could be blamed on a childhood cold, a reaction to an injection or simple good spirits. At 13, it was a lot harder to excuse. Everyone knew they had to think carefully when they chose Benedict's senior school. His long-suffering headmaster at Brambletye was in no doubt what was required. The wild, young Benedict needed to be tamed. He needed structure and responsibility – and he could get it at Harrow.

Tim and Wanda gave much consideration to the suggestion, and they certainly liked the idea of the famous, 400-year-old private school in northwest London. But could they afford it? Even though they worked a great deal, and always appeared to be busy with television, film and theatre projects, they didn't always earn that much. Both were well aware that acting was an incredibly precarious profession. And they both knew, like so many other actors do, that every job could be their last.

Although Tim came from a distinguished – though somewhat impoverished – naval and diplomatic family, could they really afford the school fees that might easily swallow up an average worker's entire annual wage? Two pieces of good fortune fell into their laps as they tried to make the sums add up. First, Benedict himself helped out. For once, he did what he was told and became focused on the task in hand.

He sailed through his entrance exams and won an arts scholarship that took a big slice off the yearly fees. Then, his grandmother agreed to dip into her pocket to help pay the remainder. With his parents prepared to use the savings they had built up for this very purpose, the family was ready for the transition. Just as Wanda took on one of her favourite and most famous roles – as Cassandra's mother, Pamela Parr, in the Peckham-based sitcom *Only Fools and Horses* starring David Jason and Nicholas Lyndhurst – Benedict was walking into a quite different world. He was to become part of the old-money school tradition that had given the country eight prime ministers, including Robert Peel and Winston Churchill.

The culture shock, of course, was immense, even for someone from a comfortable background like Benedict's. "I was a very middle class kid by most standards," he remembers. "I was surrounded by Lord Rothschild's son, Prince Hussein's son, dignitaries, princes and peers left, right and centre. There were those who were super rich and went off on their holidays to Aspen, while I would go and see my grandmother in Brighton. There was a disparity in what we could afford to do on our holidays."

But there was very little disparity in what the boys all did in school. Everyone had to follow the rules, muck in and take part in as many activities as possible. It was exactly what the over-active Benedict needed – just as his old Brambletye headmaster had predicted. Benedict himself remembers Harrow as the perfect combination of Hogwarts and *Swallows and Amazons*. Even though there had been some tussles at the beginning, in the end he didn't just get through the experience, he thrived on it. "It suited me down to the ground. It really was the moulding of me," he told *Daily Telegraph* reporter Benjamin Secher many years later.

Having been raised as an only child, Benedict loved the chance to make friends, and as a keen, rough and tough sportsman, he found it easy to fit in. "I was gregarious and found a coterie of brothers I'd never had before. I fell in love with the place." As an arts scholar, he spent a lot of time painting, but he spent more time on the cricket and rugby pitches. And he was always itching to go on stage, even though his early roles were somewhat embarrassing. His debut, he remembers with a throaty laugh, was in another production of *A Midsummer Night's Dream*. But this time, he wasn't cast as the comic character Bottom, he was now the fairy queen Titania. And then a little while later, he was back on stage in *As You Like It*. This times he played Rosalind. All along, he was encouraged to act on stage as a way to direct his energy somewhere other than fighting, or as he once put it, "to repress the tearaway in me."

Harrow was, he is keen to remind people, an all-boys school – someone had to play the girls' parts. And as his voice took a long time to break, that meant he was in the running for them for quite some time. Fortunately, the ribbing from the other boys didn't last for long. Being a fighter and being so good at rugby helped. As did the fact that he wasn't messing around on stage. Even as a teenager, Benedict's attitude to drama was strikingly serious. If he was playing the part of a woman, then he would play it to the very best of his ability. And it showed. "My Rosalind was deemed by my drama teacher as the finest since Vanessa Redgrave's," he laughs. It's a joke, of course. But there's truth in it. That same drama teacher, Martin Tyrell, has called Benedict "the best schoolboy actor I've worked with." And once his voice broke, and as he shot towards his current height of just over six feet, he got the chance to play an even broader range of parts.

Harrow typically produces about 20 plays per academic year, which provided plenty of opportunities for Benedict to participate in theatre. He took on several character roles, played several old men, and was particularly good as the iconic 60-something American Willy Loman in *Death of a Salesman*. What he called his "first big, silly role" at school was that of Arthur Crocker-Harris in Terence Rattigan's *The Browning Version*. "My job was to make schoolmasters' wives weep with recognition." He also became a great mimic. Benedict's half-sister, Tracy, remembers how his impersonations got better every year. She says he could mimic her, their parents, his teachers and even Harrow's venerable headmaster.

Two group photos taken during his years at Harrow in the early 1990s show Benedict as a blond lad with wicket-keeper hands, which represents the sporty side of Benedict's Harrow education. However, a later photo of the teenage thespian shows him wearing his "rats" tie in honour of the playwright Rattigan, who not only attended Harrow but once lived in The Park, the house where Benedict also lived as a student.

Chapter 3
Tipping the Odds

It was Benedict's final year at Harrow when Andrew Birkin, the Academy Award nominated writer and film director, visited the school. He was looking to cast his latest project, a film version of Ian McEwan's adult-themed novel *The Cement Garden*. As a former pupil himself, Birkin knew he would have the pick of the best from the school's drama students and had already asked the teaching staff to encourage the most talented pupils to come forward to audition. Benedict was one of the first to be asked, but much to everyone's surprise, he turned the opportunity down. The school was most probably as baffled as everyone else, for had he been cast, it would more than likely have propelled Benedict from complete unknown to bright new young star, and at the same time, would have been the best kick-start to a career in film that anyone could ask for.

Not only that, but star parts in films don't come along every day, especially if you don't have an agent, a showreel or any professional experience. But Benedict had his reasons. He wasn't about to appear in a movie for the sake of it, even if it did mean missing out on an opportunity to be involved with a film that was destined to become a box office hit, albeit a controversial one. It could have been just the break that he was looking for, but he didn't want any part of it. The adult themes of the story, which included incest between teenaged siblings and required nudity, made him cautious. Rather than face his insecurities or take the risk, he walked way from it. "I was really prudish at that age and I didn't want to take my clothes off. I was terrified and I didn't want anyone seeing what I looked like. So I didn't audition."

Rebecca Hall, the actress best known for her role as Caroline Cushing in Ron Howard's *Frost/Nixon* blockbuster in 2008, could understand his reluctance. She first met Benedict when she was eight and he was 14, when according to Rebecca, it was clear that he would take a while to grow into his looks. "He was one of those boys that you met, and you could already see what he was going to be like when he was middle aged," she once said with a smile. But while his looks might change, she confirmed his personality was pretty fixed. Even as a boy, he had been his own man. "He's a one-off. And he was never going to be the next anybody, he was always going to be just who he is."

It seemed the wild child who had dreamed of following in his parents' footsteps was growing up. He knew he had choices, but felt he had something to prove. It was around the same time, when he was considering his options and coming to the end of his time at Harrow, that he had his second run-in with mortality. He was at home, studying for his A-levels in his bedroom, when all of a sudden the whole flat shook from a huge explosion. The windows shattered, a dust cloud enveloped him and his ears rang. "You just thought, 'Fuck!' I ran through the flat. My mum and dad were saying 'are you all right?' I said no, I couldn't hear out of one ear." It was the 1994 terrorist attack on the Israeli Embassy, when a car packed with 14 kilograms of explosives went off and injured 30 people. Benedict remembers a deafening silence then the terrible sound of glass falling to earth.

At 18, the tall, sports-loving young man who had just escaped injury from a bomb, was looking for a completely different challenge, and in the end, he decided it wouldn't be acting. Instead, he came up with the idea to get away from it all, to find whatever he was looking for, elsewhere. That elsewhere started behind a perfume counter at the upmarket Penhaligon's perfume house in London, as well as several local restaurants where diners probably still remember being served by a tall, slightly gawkish-looking young man with an angular face and a mop of untidy, auburn hair. In both places, Benedict was trying to earn as much money as possible, as he needed to fund a gap-year trip to teach English in a Tibetan monastery – a trip he decided would be "a fantastic experience" and indeed it was. He travelled to Darjeeling, India, where as well as teaching English, Benedict was able to observe the monks at work and at prayer.

India was also where Benedict faced another near-death experience. He had got lost while hiking with friends. Armed only with a biscuit and a piece of cheese between four of them, he remembers walking across outcrops lined with ice and down semi-frozen rivers "nearly breaking our necks", poking yak droppings in the hope they were warm "to see how far we could be from some kind of civilization", and finally breaking through the tree line. Falling to his knees near the home of a Sherpa shepherd, he made the universal hand-to-mouth gesture for food. And that's when he was given a meal of spinach and meat only to get dysentery after eating it. It was, he says today, the best meal he's ever had. But the resulting illness was the third of his near misses, when he really thought he was going to die.

On his return to the UK, he recapped how he had lived rough, laughed a great deal, learned to meditate and to think for himself. Its appeal, he still says, was "the ability to focus and have a real sense of purity of purpose and attention and not be too distracted. And to feel very alive to your environment, to know what you are part of, to understand what is going on in your peripheral vision, and behind you as well as what is in front of you."

Once he had returned home to Britain, he had reached another decision. He was now considering a career in law as a barrister, which would offer him the chance of a secure position in very well paid employment. It was something that he believed would provide him with the right stability for a good lifestyle. Or so he thought. But could he really shake off the acting bug that he had already been exposed to? More importantly, could he really give up the stage and turn his back on the very thing he loved, the thing which had given his own parents so much pleasure and enjoyment? Acting was not like any other job, and working as a barrister was about as far removed as you could get from being in the showbiz limelight. After a lot of soul-searching, he realized, no, he couldn't. The more he considered the option of studying law, the more quickly he came to see that what he really wanted to do was act. And despite his parents' advice and counsel, and their offer to help him find his way around the casting and audition circuit, he turned down all offers of assistance. He wanted to do it his way or not at all.

Instead of taking the easy route and allowing his parents to help him find work, Benedict was going to learn about his craft from the basics and step out of the "privileged bubble" that had been afforded to him by his background. He headed north to study drama at the University of Manchester, still one of the largest universities in the country, with more than 50,000 students and staff squeezed into the middle of an equally busy city. He had chosen Manchester for a very simple reason, though: "I needed to be out of danger of tying a cashmere jumper round my neck. I wanted something a bit more racy, a bit more different, a bit more egalitarian." And it seems to have worked as, by his own admission, he had "a thoroughly healthy – and unhealthy – mix of friends."

He also was given a surprisingly wide range of experiences during his time of study. "We did a practical course in prisons and probation, which meant learning about the penal system and forms of rehabilitation, and then going in with a project for a month and a half to Strangeways, two other category C facilities and a probation centre." As he explains, "For a posh bloke with a silly name, to be in a world like that was extraordinary." It was useful too, and was just one of the many important experiences that could give Benedict's acting the depth he was looking for in the years to come.

Three notable things happened while Benedict was living in Manchester. The first was that he overdid things and contracted glandular fever – part of a pattern of too much work and too much stress that would return to haunt him many more times in the years ahead. Most people are only ever likely to suffer with the illness once. For it to be recurring, as in Benedict's case, would perhaps suggest other complications, such as overdoing it to the point that his immune system cannot handle extra stress or tiredness.

The second was that he met Olivia Poulet, fell in love and began a relationship that would take him through many of the turbulent times that lay ahead. Olivia was also studying drama at Manchester, and after performing with the National Youth Theatre, had started acting professionally. Her first television credit following graduation was in *The Bill* in 2001. After that, she won herself roles in *Teachers* and *Outnumbered*, and then created quite a storm in 2005, when she played the young Camilla Parker Bowles – opposite Laurence Fox as Prince Charles – in the TV royal romance *Whatever Love Means*. Most critics agreed that her portrayal of the young, sexy and horsey Camilla was perfect. Later, she played Carol Thatcher in *Margaret*, the TV biopic about Margaret Thatcher starring Lindsay Duncan, and even ended up playing a cameo role in *The Blind Banker*, the second episode of the first *Sherlock* series.

Born in Putney in southwest London, almost two years to the day after Benedict, on 9 July 1978, Olivia comes from, as she puts it, "a high-achieving clan." Her grandmother, Stella Hamilton, acted in Donald Wolfit's company, her mother is a judge and her brother Jamie is a neuroscientist in Germany. Her father was a management consultant who gave it up to sell Dinky toys on the Internet until his death from cancer in 2008. Like Benedict, Olivia began acting at school and always ended up playing the male parts at her all-girls school, Putney High, which she says was the result of her broad shoulders and height. In person, she is said to be smart, funny, and not remotely "jolly hockey sticks" as some journalists have suggested.

Today, she is best known for her stage work as well as her writing sketches and plays with comedy partner Sarah Solemani. Together they took *Bird Flu Diaries* and *The Queef of Terence* to the Edinburgh Fringe, and have since written a comedy drama for the BBC about women in their early thirties, which Olivia describes as the next stage up from *Girls*.

Like fellow actresses Miranda Hart and Catherine Tate, Olivia knows how important it is to generate her own characters. "It's a great relief when you start writing because it frees up so many things. You can write things you would want to be in, and that you believe are important for others to see." More recently, she finished writing a screenplay, *Row Girls*, based on the true story of four girls who rowed across the Atlantic. "I think it could be quite beautiful actually, as well as funny and charming. There aren't many female sports movies. It's about ambition and what could possess four people to row 3,000 miles across the Atlantic?"

The third thing to happen to Benedict while he was in Manchester was that his father came to visit when he was cast in one of the University's biggest productions. All these years later, Benedict and his dad sometimes differ about the exact play and the exact production that meant most to them. Sometimes they think it was when Benedict played Ricky Roma in the legendary *Glengarry Glen Ross* and sometimes they think it was when he was playing Salieri in *Amadeus*. Either way, they are both agreed on what happened afterwards. Benedict had put in a powerhouse performance. According to some observers, tears and emotions ran high as the two said their goodbyes in the theatre car park. And Benedict can still remember exactly what his father told him. "My dad did this extraordinary thing. He said to me, 'You are better than I ever was or will be, and you can make a living at this.' It knocked me sideways." But could it be true? Could Benedict really make a living as an actor? It seemed he could.

Decision time came just before graduation day. And having missed out on the chance of an early film role in his final days at Harrow, Benedict looked set to miss out on many more opportunities over the next year. For he decided he wasn't ready to look for fulltime work and stood back as slightly younger contemporaries and friends such as *The Last King of Scotland* and *Wanted* star James McAvoy hit the audition circuit and began to win lead roles. Benedict turned the opportunities and the money down and decided to stay in training for at least another 12 months.

"He knew acting was something you had to work hard at," said set designer Michael Holt who supervised Benedict's dissertation at

Manchester University. Holt fully understood when the youngster applied for a one-year course at LAMDA, the west-London-based Academy of Music and Dramatic Art that has produced everyone from Maureen Lipman to *Poirot* star David Suchet. LAMDA's big selling point is its intensely practical course work – and its very tough work ethic. Students are encouraged to focus on the reality of working in the entertainment industry and to prepare for a long, tough slog on the audition trail. Benedict thrived on the real-life lessons he learned there. And he loved the acting classes. He paid his dues, refined his craft – and then had a rare lapse of professional judgement.

The error came when he tried to find an agent. The self-proclaimed "posh bloke with a silly name" had decided that his highbrow background might count against him. His father had given up the Cumberbatch name to win work, so Benedict decided to do the same. He would get shot of his three-syllable first name at the same time. So as his graduation from LAMDA approached, Benedict reinvented himself as plain old Ben Carlton.

Ben Carlton, of course, has never been heard of since. His agent put the snappy-sounding young man up for all sorts of parts. He read in front of all sorts of people. But he didn't get anywhere. After a few fruitless months, Ben decided to find a different agent – and the first thing they talked about was his full, unwieldy name. Much to his surprise, the agent liked it. "My new agent suggested I revert," he remembers. "I thought Benedict Cumberbatch sounded a bit bumbly and messy, but they said it was a great name and that it would get people talking about me."

Benedict was still not convinced. "How much is it going to cost to put my name in lights?" he asked. Then he decided that wasn't his problem. If the hotshot new agent thought the six-syllable Benedict Cumberbatch name would work, then Benedict Cumberbatch it would be. And if the name ever went up in lights, then he would be too ecstatic to worry about the cost or the carbon footprint.

And so, after this latest re-launch and several years after his false starts following Harrow and Manchester University, Benedict was ready to test himself. He got a role almost immediately, a bit-part in the long-running TV series *Heartbeat*, a classic first step for any hungry actor and the kind of bread-and-butter work his parents had made their own over the years.

But it was not until the summer of 2001, when newcomer Benedict was a relatively long-in-the-tooth 25, that he got his first real break. He was cast in the company at the Open Air Theatre in London's Regent Park. It was a glorious setting for Shakespeare – though actors can be beaten by the weather, and sometimes have to fight to be heard over the sound of distant car alarms and low-flying planes. Benedict was playing the King of Navarre in *Love's Labour's Lost* and Demetrius in *A Midsummer Night's Dream*. They were big roles that have been played by countless actors over the years. So it is all the more incredible that Benedict, in his professional debut, played the roles so differently and won so much acclaim. He admits he could barely believe it himself when he was nominated for the year's Best Classical Stage Performance in the 2001 Ian Charleson Awards.

Benedict finally appeared to be on his way. But he still took some hard knocks. One night, his old fragilities resurfaced. He lost his voice and had to let his understudy take to the stage in his place. To this day he remembers cycling home in tears as he beat himself up for letting so many people down. But had he really?

The incident didn't stop him being asked to rejoin the Open Air Company for the 2002 summer season, where he sang his heart out in the musical *Oh! What A Lovely War!* When he wasn't in the park, Benedict auditioned for any and every part going, winning a few more minor roles in TV shows like crime drama *Silent Witness* and the controversial BBC drama about lesbian love, *Tipping the Velvet*. During this period it looked as if Benedict's career was going to mirror that of his parents, as he managed to drift in and out of minor roles in a host of well-known shows and did some well-regarded theatre. He worked a great deal, but never quite hit the heights. But then, at the age of 28 and out of the blue, Benedict won the role of his life, to play physicist Stephen Hawking. That was the moment when he started to leave his parents behind. It was also when the true madness began.

Chapter 4

A Taste of Hollywood

When the BBC announced its forthcoming biography of Stephen Hawking, there were many who wondered if the 90-minute drama was going to be a tough sell. Could there be any drama in the life of a physicist? Would viewers really want to watch the story of a character whose body is gradually being taken over by motor neurone disease? And wasn't it in bad taste to portray the physical decline of someone who was still very much alive? It seemed it wasn't. Hawking's story is, after all, one of survival. It is the tale of a bright and ambitious 21-year-old PhD student at Cambridge University who is diagnosed with the debilitating motor neurone disease, given two years to live and then, against all odds, goes on to achieve scientific success and worldwide acclaim.

Even so, when Benedict summarized the premise of *Hawking*, there were still those who doubted its appeal as a TV film. But as Benedict explained, it was "a story of hope, without a doubt, and a story of grace under pressure, how to conquer adversity and how a situation like that can be used for the positive. He's a small person with an incredible brain in a very fragile body, thinking incredible, huge thoughts."

Interestingly enough, Benedict's audition placed him streets ahead of the other actors being considered for the role for one very simple reason. He could speak the way Hawking spoke. "The voice, funnily enough, I picked up very quickly, and apparently I was the first in the audition to give it a crack. It was quite clearly written in the script. It's slightly like the atonal palate of a deaf person because the soft palate goes, the atonal variation goes, the tongue loses its elasticity so it's very vowelly, the consonants go," he explained, when Nicola Christie caught up with him for an April 2004 interview in *The Times*. Then Benedict joked that the voice was similar to his own when he suffers a hangover. This was typical of his interview style – he often explains a character or his process in depth, but then adds a joke as if he is worried that he may be too serious for his audience. His responses, however, illustrate to anyone who is not an actor, exactly how he approaches an audition or develops a character he is playing.

For *Hawking*, one of the first things Benedict did in his preparation for the role was to meet with Stephen, read books about his work and work with a LAMDA movement coach. "It was terrifying meeting him," admits Benedict. "He's such a presence and you have to really know what you want to say to him, or ask him, because it takes such a huge, phenomenal effort for him to communicate with you. You think 'I really don't want to waste his time.'"

Benedict also made contact with the Motor Neurone Disease Association and met two people with very different degrees of MND. They allowed him to film them so he could try to mirror the way the condition affected their movements. They also talked him through their own experiences. "They were remarkably brave in their frankness and honesty about how it started, and what they had felt emotionally and physically."

Certainly some actors like to joke that their jobs are actually quite simple. "All you have to do is remember your lines and don't walk into furniture," they claim. But playing Stephen wasn't quite that simple for Benedict. In several scenes for *Hawking*, he had to stand at the blackboard feverishly chalking scientific symbols all over it – and he had to get them right. "The people who know them work in split seconds and even on TV screens, they'll pick up an inconsistency. It was very, very hard," he remembers. His other challenge, he admits, was "not to let the symptoms swamp the character" he was playing.

With only one week of rehearsal before shooting began, Benedict felt that "every day there would be something else I'd get a bit more right, and feel more confident about." For the fearsome task of learning how to quickly write quotations across a board, Benedict says he was enormously helped by a pupil of Stephen's who worked on the production and "drew stuff out for me to have a look at the night before." On screen, it was quite remarkable to watch how Benedict made illustrating Hawking's thought process look easy. It was, say observers, all part of his theatrical brilliance.

Although the memorization of scientific theory may have daunted Benedict, other scenes, beyond the mastery of movement or maths, reveal highly impressive aspects of his craft. In one scene, during Hawking's twenty-first birthday party, the young man slips away with the woman who will one day become his wife, and the two stretch out side by side on the lawn to look up at the night sky. Hawking amiably discusses the physics of stars. The romantic idyll is shattered when, deciding it's time to return to the party, Hawking makes the horrific discovery that he cannot stand up. Benedict's voice conveys a huge emotional range, from discovery to embarrassment, to fear and panic.

After a series of painful tests, Hawking confronts his doctor and demands to know the results. He refuses to wait until his parents arrive to hear the news and is therefore standing alone in a hospital ward while the doctor explains the progression of motor neurone disease. Benedict's face, as Hawking, completely reflects and captures the scientist's realization that his brain will survive untouched, but that the rest of his body will shut down. As in other performances, Benedict excels in the ability to reveal a character's thoughts and emotions in key scenes that often lack dialogue. It is probably true to say that *Hawking* was the first widely seen performance to show this particular aspect of Benedict's acting style and ability.

It is also probably true, no matter how good or bad the appeal of the drama was, that no one expected it to top the ratings when it aired on 13 April 2004. Much of its success, however, lies with Benedict himself. Even in pre-production, everyone knew that if the actor chosen to play the lead role wasn't up to the job, then the film would sink without trace. Ask any film or TV critic today, and they are likely to tell you that the reason the drama turned out to be so successful was down to Benedict. Once again, he had proved that it pays to do your homework. Not that his method of preparation was any surprise to his publicist, Karon Maskill. Some years after *Hawking* was screened, she confirmed that her client was renowned for going the extra mile whenever he won a new part. "He does a great deal of preparation before each of his roles, both physical and mental, and by the time he reaches the set he is totally under the skin of the person he is playing, and brings a great deal of emotional intelligence to bear."

Even if the drama wasn't a mainstream hit, it was a critical success, and it didn't go unnoticed in the plethora of awards shows with which the film and television industry now abounds. Not for the last time in his career, Benedict was nominated for a BAFTA Best Actor award and even though he was only narrowly pipped at the post by *Notting Hill*'s Rhys Ifans, it was still an incredible achievement considering it was Benedict's first major lead role. As a rising star, his other challenge was to meet the press and give some interviews, something he was not used to. At first, the press wasn't quite sure what to make of him. Patricia Nicol from *The Times* was one of the first to interview him. "He has the angry, gingery, wide-eyed features of a marketeer caught on the hop," she wrote. And another reporter, from *The Sunday Times*, was even more unsettled by him. "As Stephen Hawking, his body has closed down. In real life, this man cannot sit still." That comment could have equally summed up Benedict's attitude to life at the time. As a boy he had always appeared to be in a hurry, but as a man, he seemed to be in a crazy rush. It was something his agent agreed with. If nothing else, Benedict was always more than happy to audition for almost any work that was up for grabs. He would juggle dates to try and appear in as many productions as possible. And however tired he got, he would always give auditions his best shot.

But, not everything appeared to be plain sailing. Spending a couple of hours sweating through a dinner jacket while doing stunts in a shabby, overheated Soho office in 2004 at a casting call for a video game version of James Bond was not Benedict's idea of fun. Being turned down for the role didn't bother him that much, because by then Benedict was already committed to another project and was about to board a plane to South Africa. It was his first big-budget location shoot, but he had no idea that it would turn into such a nightmare and put his own life on the line.

The project couldn't have come at a better time. In the months leading up to filming, in 2004, he had become concerned that his career was not taking the path he thought it should. Even though he had made a brief return to the set of *Heartbeat* and had won a few one-off roles in shows like *Cambridge Spies* and *Spooks*, he wasn't being offered any major TV parts and was starting to feel assailed by self-doubt. He wondered if his accent was too plummy for mainstream TV? Was his face too angular for a leading man? Would he have to grow into his looks as Rebecca

Hall had predicted, and would he have to wait years before he found solid work as a character actor? The concerns grew stronger as he slogged away in theatres and on the casting trail. Not that he would have to worry for long. All his doubts soon fell away when he landed the lead role in David Attwood's three-part adaptation of William Golding's acclaimed sea trilogy *To the Ends of the Earth*, which premiered on BBC 2 in July 2005, almost one year after filming had been completed. According to Benedict, it was "a sort of rock-and-roll 1812 period drama about a young man's gap year! It's full of filth, dirt, discovery, sex, drugs, dancing, love, spiritual awakenings and massive sweeping changes." Based on Golding's three acclaimed novels *Rites of Passage*, *Close Quarters* and *Fire Down Below*, the mini-series charted in visceral detail the rites-of-passage story of Edmund Talbot, a young English aristocrat as he experiences life on board a passenger ship making its hazardous voyage from England to Australia in the early nineteenth century.

The idea of turning the books into a mini-series for television was the brainchild of television director and production manager David Attwood. "I read the first book, *Rites of Passage*, in 1980 and I remember thinking then, 'God, some mad idiot might try and make a film of this and it would be almost impossible to do,' but when I was asked if I'd be interested, I said 'yes'. I liked the ineffable bigness of William Golding as a novelist, it's a mature and intelligent piece of writing that can be funny, ribald, sexy, mad, violent and dangerous. It is all those things, but it is also an examination of what people do to each other in a claustrophobic situation. It's an epic, but at the heart of it, is an extremely detailed and microscopic view of human nature."

Golding, who was awarded the Nobel Prize for literature in 1983 and is best known for his first novel, *Lord of the Flies*, wrote his sea trilogy towards the end of his life. It helped that he had an all-encompassing knowledge of the sea – he was a naval commander during the Second World War and became a passionate amateur sailor after the war ended. Attwood's first choice of writer to adapt the novels was Leigh Jackson, who jumped at the chance but died before he could finish the third novel, or indeed before the film got into production. "It was a great partnership with Leigh and it was an absolute tragedy that he fell ill while we were working together," says Attwood. "He had done a massive amount of work on the first episode, and quite a lot on the second and third. He was still working hard at it up until the last week of his life, with incredible tenacity, courage and amazing humour. He loved this project and he wanted it to carry on. After Leigh died, we turned to Tony Basgallop, who brought his own significant contribution and his own individual voice to the project. I think Leigh would have been very happy with what Tony has done. In fact, they could have worked together. We dedicated the films to Leigh because they are very much in his spirit."

Attwood's qualifications for bringing a sea epic to the screen weren't just down to his considerable abilities as a director. "I've been across the Atlantic about seven times, I've done cargo ships and I've crewed on yachts. The journey itself is just an extraordinary thing to do, in all weather, so from the very smallest boats to quite large ships, I've been in quite big storms and I don't think I'd ever seen them portrayed accurately. The sea is unpredictable and difficult and changeable, all the things that filming hopefully isn't."

Benedict, of course, was thrilled to join the production, and to be cast alongside Sam Neill, Jared Harris, Victoria Hamilton, Charles Dance, Joanna Page, Paula Jennings, Denise Black and Theo Landey. Attwood was equally thrilled. "We found Benedict fairly early. We needed a very good actor, someone young enough to be believable as an aristocratic, an almost slightly dislikeable character who is an adolescent in terms of his views of the world, his upbringing. But we also needed someone who could hold the screen for four and a half hours, in every scene. We needed someone with experience who was not only a very good actor, but also with terrific comic timing. Benedict was the ideal answer to that."

Producer Lynn Horsford agrees. "Benedict was remarkable. He carried the Golding novels with him on set and constantly referred to them. We needed him every single day and he just didn't stop, nor complain. He simply became Edmund Talbot. And that commitment spread to every cast member. The process of making this film echoed the journey the characters went on in the story, and we really got to know each other during our four months on location and we became very close."

That closeness wasn't just confined to the time on set. Outside of filming, Benedict explained, "we had the most extraordinary time. The cast had great fun together. We had poker nights, beach parties, dune buggying, horseback safaris. One weekend we went to a game reserve called Phinda, where we were treated like royalty and had our own cook. It was really posh and the most expensive treat I gave myself during filming. I then learned to scuba dive in one of the most beautiful places on God's Earth, about a three-hour drive from where we were filming. I'd already been whale watching, but on my second dive I swam with a whale that was about 10 feet away from me. It was magical, the most beautiful sight; there was a baby whale swimming by its head. When I finished filming in Cape Town, I went swimming with great white sharks. I was in a cage and they were fed just beside us. It was terrifying and wonderful; they are such a potent force of nature."

Taking on the role of Edmund Talbot, however, was quite a commitment. As Lynn Horsford has already pointed out, he would appear in virtually every scene and would be on set every day, throughout the four-month shoot on location in South Africa. "Every day was different and, ultimately, that was the greatest gift of this job," raved Benedict. "The hours were exhausting but each day was a new challenge. I loved hurling myself round that boat on ropes, bits of rigging falling around me in flames, with the contrast of filming the intimacy of the cabin scenes. Edmund has a massive learning curve throughout the three books. I always brought the books on set as a reference point. He is incredibly confident, a little bit arrogant, vulnerable and always open to learning. He's very much a product of his time and class. An establishment figure, he has all the airs and graces of his social position. He is full of ambition, wilful, always thinks he's in control and permanently confounded. And he's moody and neurotic, but he's got a good sense of humour. Above all else, I was very keen to make him sympathetic. I didn't want him to be just someone who was a product of his class, but more a fully rounded, three-dimensional human being. Golding's books expose him at every level as a fallible young man."

The books also provided excellent source material for Benedict to get under the skin of his character to the degree where, by the end of the shoot, his fellow cast members were calling him Edmund and not Ben. One great challenge he had to face during filming, however, was the shooting of his first-ever on-screen sex scene, with Paula Jennings playing Zenobia. "My on-screen sex technique is not perfected but I hope it worked! In the book, Edmund knows what he's doing and maybe that's him writing himself up in his journal as a bit of a lothario, but I imagine that rather like others of his ilk, his father had probably given him a chambermaid or prostitute to initiate him. He behaves with Zenobia like a sexual animal, he's very avaricious and knowing. He's charming and flirts with her from the very first day he sees her, and he goes straight for the kill."

Filming itself, was not without it problems. It was crucial to the success of the drama that the correct decisions about where to film were made. Risking the unpredictable British weather was not an option, especially as it would be necessary to create the illusion of the boat crossing to the southern hemisphere. "If you're doing a 'Boy's Own' story it doesn't matter whether it's raining or calm," admits Attwood, "but in *To the Ends of the Earth*, the weather and what happens to the ship is integral to what happens to the characters. One of the things I needed to have as director was control of the weather, which of course is the most difficult thing to control."

The climate was one of the reasons why Richard's Bay (three hours north of Durban) in South Africa was chosen as a location. "A lot of this story happens near the equator or in the doldrums, south of the equator. We needed calm weather and some sunshine, but we also needed storms and all the variations you get of weather at sea – drizzle, grey days, choppy days, Channel weather, big ocean swells. They all have an effect on the story. So although it seems a crazy and megalomaniac to say 'I've got to be in charge of the weather on this,' that had to be part of our thinking."

Things, however, didn't always go to plan. As Horsfield recalls, the crew "experienced some of the worst weather they'd had in years, even making headlines in the local press. That had a big impact on our schedule. We were in a very beautiful location, but filming at sea is always a nightmare. The sea is either too rough or too still. Just getting the cast and crew and all our equipment on the ship each day was a major operation."

Attwood agrees with this view: "People want to see intelligent drama and intelligent television. Our characters are confined in a claustrophobic atmosphere and you get to know them intensely over an elongated period of time. Thanks to Golding, they are people in whom you have a strong and opinionated interest. They are worried whether they are going to survive the journey, survive the storms, have to fight a sea battle, go to war. Are they going to be seasick for nine months, are they going to die? People are stuck with each other on this ship. But the characters are a wonderful cross section of different aspects of British and European society and in them we see ourselves. In this drama we see the worst, the pettiest, the smallest aspect of ourselves, but we also see the noblest aspects of human beings."

When the finished work was shown on the BBC in the UK, PBS in America, and around the world, it won rave reviews, and once again, much of the praise was for Benedict. As one reviewer noted, "The undisputed star of the three-part drama is Cumberbatch, who is on screen in nearly every frame. He plays Edmund Talbot, an occasionally priggish aristocratic ingénue and is the sometime narrator and developing conscience. Cumberbatch's face is the shifting canvas on which Talbot's responses and reactions are registered."

Of course, we know about the terrifying events that occurred during a break in filming, when Benedict, Denise and Theo headed out on the road for some downtime. We also know that after recovering from the ordeal in London, he was determined to grab every chance that came his way. It seems the first opportunity that he considered worth seizing, almost one year later in 2005, was a return to the London stage at the trendy Almeida Theatre in Islington, where he would appear from 10 March to 30 April playing George Tesman, the cuckolded husband in Henrik Ibsen's *Hedda Gabler*. After that, the show would transfer to the Duke of York's Theatre in London's West End, running for almost three months from 19 May to 6 August. For some actors, moving from theatre to theatre in the middle of a run can be irritating, but not for Benedict. He was happy to adapt providing the new venue was suitable, and in this case it was. Even more remarkable was his knowledge about the importance of a theatre. "The Almeida is a theatre, not a studio. It has been adapted into a space that's intimate but very much on a theatre principle. The Duke of York's is in the theatre bijou style. It's typically Victorian with a proscenium arch. The move will certainly present new challenges, but I don't think we'll lose the level of intimacy. If we were playing to one of the bigger houses in the West End, that might be a problem, but the space that's been chosen should work very well."

Widely condemned when it first appeared in 1890, *Hedda Gabler* has since become one of Ibsen's most frequently performed dramas. The role of Hedda is a complex one, for she is a strong and intelligent woman trapped in the stuffy and confined world of late nineteenth-century bourgeois society. Afraid of being judged, Hedda opts for a conventional but loveless marriage in which she quickly becomes bored. By blending comedy and tragedy, Ibsen explores the frustrated aspirations of his characters against a background of contemporary social mores.

At the start of the play, Hedda is seen returning home after an extended honeymoon; already she is bored with married life, finding it devoid of pleasure or adventure. Hedda now strives to find a means of breaking free from this existence and rekindling her passion for life – in doing so, she seeks to manipulate those around her. It was another of Isben's characteristic takes on defining characters and their struggles, and the inner conflicts that beset all human beings. Certainly, Isben is one of Benedict's favourite playwrights. Two years before *Hedda Gabler*, he had played Lyngstrand in Trevor Nunn's 2003 Almeida production of Ibsen's *The Lady From the Sea*, which starred Natasha Richardson in the title role. When comparing the two roles, Benedict noted, "there are similarities, of course – as well as the fact that both characters are naïve men who have rude awakenings. In Tesman's case, the awakening is a far more dramatic and forceful one – it's done my ego no good at all! At the end of each week, I have to check Eve Best still likes me. Being an emotional punch bag for eight performances a week takes its toll. But I've enjoyed the work for different reasons. The frail physicality of *The Lady from the Sea*'s Lyngstrand – and his age and level of experience – required a very different interpretation to that of Tesman. So, even though on paper Tesman and Lyngstrand seem similar characters, if you held the two performances up, you'd see they are very different. I don't want to bore myself or my audience."

One of the most revealing aspects of Benedict at work during the production of the play was an image that photographer Simon Annand captured for his book and photo exhibition of actors preparing for the stage. It pictured Benedict as a thinker, checking props in the moments before going on stage. With one hand Benedict holds his suit jacket in place while the other hand checks his coat pocket for a prop. He is looking down, and his attitude is relaxed. This is a man simply doing his job, ensuring that he is ready to go stage. He does not seem rushed or concerned, merely attentive. In the background of the small dressing room are the usual real-life props: photographs on the wall, a mirror surrounded by bright bulbs and an almost empty water bottle capped on the table, is if the actor had just been drinking from it.

What is perhaps interesting, though, is how the production of *Hedda Gabler* came about. Director Richard Eyre says it was inspired by something he saw in *Hello!* magazine. He had picked up a copy in his dentist's waiting room and read an interview "with a rich, posh young woman who was celebrated for being celebrated." In the interview, she confessed, without irony, to "having a great talent for boredom" to which Eyre's response was "Mmmm, Hedda Gabler lives." That same evening he went to see Howard Davies's production of Eugene O'Neill's *Mourning Becomes Electra* at the National, in which Eve Best gave such a thrilling performance that Eyre realized she was born to play Hedda. The rest, as they say, is theatrical history.

When Benedict applied for the part of Hedda Gabler's husband George Tesman and got it, he was literally thrilled, even if he was, as he put it, slightly scared. "I wanted the challenge of making Tesman a sympathetic, three-dimensional character and to give him the integrity that is often overlooked, to try to honour Ibsen's intentions. Tesman has a genuine love of his wife born out of respect. Hedda is above him socially and he wants to be a worthy match for her. He hero-worships her, thinks she's fantastic, beautiful and a great catch." As some observers noted, Benedict played Tesman sincerely, as an academic so bound up with his work that he fails to notice his wife is bored. He tries so hard to please his new bride that he pushes aside his own feelings until they can be suppressed no longer. In a pivotal scene, when Benedict as Tesman realizes that his wife has done something terrible in order to protect him and to ensure no one is above him in his profession, his rapid shift of emotion had the critics raving about his performance. It was, agreed most, a truly honest and believable portrayal. For some critics though, it didn't quite ring the bell. As far as they were concerned, Benedict had to overcome perceived miscasting, and on a further downside, it was said that not everyone understood his interpretation of the character he was playing. Some even suggested that the play had drawn attention because it was the first after the Almeida's refurbishment and more critics than usual had come to see the production simply because they wanted to see the remodelled theatre.

Not that it mattered what the doomsayers said, as overall, Benedict's performance was considered to be a standout achievement. Even though Eve Best garnered most of the attention and Benedict's performance wasn't quite enough to win him the Olivier Best Supporting Actor nomination he was up for, it was sufficiently good for him to walk away with the Ian Charleson Award for Best Classical Stage Performance – something he is still very proud of to this day.

He was equally proud of his decision to accept a role in the coming-of-age drama that was being executive-produced by Tom Hanks and bankrolled by his production company, Playtone. They had already optioned the film rights to the David Nicholls book *Starter For Ten* on which the film was based, and started looking for a suitable director to take the reins in bringing the book to the screen. It had, after all, become an instant must-read hit of the year, was selected as a Richard & Judy Book Club choice and went on to sell over 300,000 copies. Recognizing in the story some of the qualities present in the his own buoyant coming-of-age directorial debut, *That Thing You Do*, in 1996 Hanks shared the script with

American Beauty and *Road to Perdition* director Sam Mendes, who in turn suggested they co-produce the film and stay true to the book by shooting in England with an all-British cast. And indeed that is what they did.

The story focuses on a working-class student from Essex during his first year at Bristol University. Brian Jackson, played by McAvoy, has a lot to prove. While his hometown mates worry about him turning into a ponce, Brian's biggest concern is making the team for the long-running television quiz show *University Challenge*, which sees four-member teams from posh universities competing against each other. Amidst Tarts & Vicars dances, anti-Apartheid rallies and puffs of marijuana smoke, Brian also finds himself romantically torn between two very different women: ultra-fit, blonde beauty and *University Challenge* team-mate Alice (Alice Eve, who coincidentally, would years later, star alongside Benedict in *Star Trek Into Darkness*), and thoughtful, politically aware Rebecca Epstein (Rebecca Hall). Set against Margaret Thatcher's economically depressed Britain, and complemented by a great soundtrack featuring music by The Cure, Wham, Bananarama, Yaz, The Smiths, New Order, Tears For Fears, Echo and the Bunnymen, The Buzzcocks and The Psychedelic Furs in the foreground, *Starter for Ten* had seemed like it was destined for great things.

By chance, a BBC producer suggested the director Tom Vaughan, knowing he had worked well with Nicholls before on the TV productions *Cold Feet* and *I Saw You*. "What delighted me was the fact that I was making my first movie on a subject that felt so close to me, that was so personal to me," says Vaughan.

"While I'm not a writer myself, I do feel very personally close to David's writing, and as a director you need to feel a certain amount of ownership of the movie even if you haven't written it." When asked about the challenges of adapting his own novel for the screen, Nicholls admits, "You take a deep breath and accept you're going to lose some things you love. The novel is written in the first person, and I originally thought it was un-adaptable because it's so much about main character Brian Jackson's voice. I think it's quite rare to have a very funny voice-over in a film, so the biggest rule I set myself when adapting was never to include a voice-over if it wasn't necessary to moving the plot forward, if it was just a joke or a passage I loved from the book."

Starter for Ten was filmed over eight weeks on location in London, Bristol and Jaywick. One of the high points of shooting involved recreating the *University Challenge* television set from 1985 using specifications provided by Granada Television. As well as its realistic set, the film boasted actor Mark Gatiss (who would later become one of the minds and writers behind *Sherlock*), a dead ringer for the show's original host, Bamber Gascoigne. He scored big laughs with British audiences during the film's morally complicated climax. For scenes set in Brian's hometown on the Essex coast, Vaughan and company moved the production to Jaywick, an English coastal town that had never hosted a film crew before (nor had the local pub, Never Say Die, been subjected to an open-to-the-public night shoot). "I wanted to get a sense of the geographic contrast between these two places," explains the director. "One is all about the horizon, the university is very vertical and intimidating. I didn't want to draw attention to the camera and wanted to maintain a naturalistic shooting style – a film like *Gregory's Girl* is very appealing to me in terms of its style of filmmaking, innocence and charm – but I did want the viewer to understand on a deep, visual level, the contrast between where this character comes from and where he's going."

The actor playing that character – one of the first to be cast – was Benedict's old ally and career nemesis, James McAvoy. Hailed in 2006 by director Kevin Macdonald as the world's "best British actor under 30 without question," McAvoy's talent for playing flawed yet sympathetic characters made him an actor to watch.

"What James brings to the film is a kind of X-factor, which makes you care about him even when he's doing something cringeworthy," says Vaughan. "He walks the line being a young guy making mistakes and keeping you on his side. You know what he's striving for, and I think James could identify with that." Nicholls agrees: "James manages to make the character likable in a way I wasn't sure he always was on the page. He makes terrible mistakes and has terrible failings, but you see the essential goodness of his intentions even if he goes about things in a foolish way. Even before he opens his mouth he brings an amiability and likeability that's immensely appealing. I remember seeing James for the first time on TV some time ago and thinking instantly that he's exceptional and is going to be a big star. He's my dream casting, really, I can't think of anyone else for the role. He's also just about the most committed, hardworking, serious actor that I've ever worked with." But according to some, if you watch *Starter*

For Ten on DVD today, it's Benedict who steals the film. What is perhaps strange, though, is that in the production notes for the film, Benedict is hardly mentioned and there is nothing about the character he plays.

Although the film picked up some excellent reviews from the critics alongside its encouraging notices from early film festival audiences, it was one of those movies that fell completely flat when it went on general release. *The Times* described it as "a terrific *Desert Island Discs* film for the 1980s... One of those rare bitter-sweet comedies that scores winners on every level." *Arena Magazine* said much the same: "The most refreshing, painfully funny comedy in years," while *Empire* applauded it as "the smartest romantic comedy of the year" and *Total Film* shouted how utterly delightful it was, "a cross between *About a Boy* and *The Breakfast Club*." Yet it only grossed a fraction of its production budget before it was withdrawn from cinemas and disappeared without trace, despite there being no real reason for it to fail at the box office.

Despite the disappointment, Benedict probably wasn't too worried. He had already moved on to his next movie project, and one that he considered had enormous commercial appeal. His zeal, it seemed, was matched by his ambition for the film to succeed. *Amazing Grace* would tell the story of the campaign against the slave trade in the British Empire, led by William Wilberforce, who was responsible for steering anti-slave trade legislation through the British parliament. The film also recounted the experiences of John Newton as a crewman on a slave ship and his subsequent religious conversion, which inspired his writing of the poem later used in the hymn. Newton is portrayed as a major influence on Wilberforce and the abolition movement.

The film premiered on 16 September 2006 at the Toronto Film Festival, followed by showings at the Heartland Film Festival, the Santa Barbara International Film Festival and the European Film Market. It opened for wide US release on 23 February 2007, a date that coincided with the 200th anniversary of the day the British parliament voted to ban the slave trade. It made over $20 million at the American box office and ended up with a respectable $32 million worldwide; on its opening weekend in February 2007, it became the tenth highest grossing film for that weekend behind such new releases as *The Astronaut Farmer* and *The Number 23*. The movie also boasted stellar casting. Ioan Gruffudd, one of the few actors with a name as complicated as Benedict's, was selected to play anti-slavery abolitionist William Wilberforce, while Benedict took on the role of prime minister William Pitt the Younger. Meanwhile, Albert Finney took the part of John Newton and Michael Gambon was cast as Charles James Fox, all of whom, shouted the critics, gave electrifying performances. For Benedict, though, it meant a great deal more. As we have already discovered, he now sees his role in the film as a means of an apology for his ancestors. This was something he would revisit years later when he took the part of a slave owner in the multi-award nominated *12 Years a Slave*.

Within a few months of *Amazing Grace* playing over 315 screens across the UK, Benedict was about to be seen for a second time in another period drama, Joe Wright's film of Ian McEwan's *Atonement*. However, this time he only had a cameo role, which despite very little screen time left an indelible impression on the critics and cinema-going public alike. Ryan Gilbey was one of those critics. Writing in the *New Statesman*, he couldn't praise Benedict's performance enough. "His chilling cameo as a predatory spiv was a sliver of a part but it informed the rest of the picture, and not only because the actions of Cumberbatch's character had a cataclysmic effect on the narrative. It was also to do with the breadth of interior life that he brought to the part: every gesture and twitch and inflection contributed to our sense that the character was pursuing his own pleasures far beyond the confines of the film we were watching. I wouldn't be so foolhardy as to attempt to distil the essence of great acting, but an aspect of it must surely be to convince us that the character lives on outside this one film or play or television show. Anyway, Cumberbatch stole *Atonement* for me." He probably stole the film for many others too.

For Benedict, the role was what the *Guardian* later termed one of his "small parts in big films." Certainly his moments on screen playing the cad and rapist of *Atonement*, was as Ryan Gilbey had already noted, suavely menacing. Although it was only a small part, it was totally pivotal in the tale of pre-Second World War loss of innocence, and the sequence of events that condemns one young man for the crime committed by another.

As with many films of this nature, the movie was hyped to win several Academy Awards, but of its six nominations, including Best Picture, it achieved only the Oscar for Best Original Score. It performed better on its home territory where it won the coveted Best Picture honour at the British Academy Awards. All the same, by that time, it had already won a great deal of Hollywood attention – especially for stars Keira Knightley, James McAvoy and newcomer Saoirse Ronan – after being feted at film festivals from Venice to Vancouver. *Variety* praised the film's lead performers and heralded *Atonement* as "both a ravishing period romance and sophisticated narrative puzzle."

Benedict frequently strode the red carpet, especially at the London premiere where he received a great deal of attention from the media. His association with a major film receiving accolades from around the world helped to create a higher industry profile. If it didn't quite propel him towards film stardom, what the attention did do was to bring him to the notice of future *Sherlock* producer Sue Vertue and one of the show's creators Steven Moffat. Having seen *Atonement*, they thought only of Benedict when they were casting their Sherlock Holmes.

Although critics and film buffs often trace Benedict's later film success back to his breakthrough performance in *Sherlock*, perhaps his stardom can be attributed more accurately to his well-received role in *Atonement*. If that is true, isn't it strange that when Benedict could have had Hollywood at his feet, he decided to do the opposite of what everyone expected? Rather than answer the beckoning calls of film producers, he chose to settle for the stage of a tiny London theatre instead.

Chapter 5
Upwards and Sideways

The Royal Court on Sloane Square in west London was the eclectic stage that had premiered works by Bertolt Brecht, Jean Sartre and Samuel Beckett, as well as giving the world the first performance of *The Rocky Horror Picture Show*. It was where Benedict's father had performed in the 1960s when he appeared in *A Patriot for Me* and *The Knack*. So it was hardly surprising that 40 years later, Benedict was keen to come full circle and bring the Cumberbatch family back to the famous venue.

Just like his dad, Benedict signed up for post-show talks with audiences, in which he discussed his roles and the political nature of both *Rhinoceros* and *The Arsonists*. Playing his roles in revolving rep with one play following the other was tough going, and once again, Benedict's body didn't always seem up to the task. He developed a stomach ulcer early on in the run, though he was proud to have kept working through the worst of it. If you had looked very carefully at him from the stalls at this point, you might have noticed a mark, almost like a tattoo, around his upper lip. It had first appeared just before the carjacking in South Africa. Dermatologists told him it was a form of skin damage and an indication of high oestrogen levels, sometimes seen in men with cancer. Having had tests to prove he was clear of the disease, Benedict was able to laugh it off, even when pals spotted the mark and accused him of wearing make-up off stage as well as on.

Both plays received mixed reviews and were deemed somewhat controversial, and reviews for Benedict himself weren't much better. No matter what the critics thought of each play, though, or indeed of Benedict's overall performance, he still shone in at least one difficult scene in each production. Certainly in *Rhinoceros*, the actor took his complacent character to emotional new heights that also revealed his physical dexterity as well as his ability to play comedy.

The higher Benedict's profile rose, the more his appearance went under the media microscope, although he had no more vanity than the usual actor or the metrosexual male in London. "His looks hint at something extraterrestrial," wrote Emma John in the *Observer*. That same weekend, *The Sunday Times* declared that he was "far from one of the pretty boys," and that "his looks are too striking and unusual to make him the sort of Romeo pin-up who pens a movie. He has exotic cheekbones, slanting blue-green eyes, a retrousse nose, thick hair and the most lavishly accentuated upper lip since 'It' girl Clara Bow. But add it all up, and you get a surprisingly attractive package." Attractive or not, Benedict, by his own admittance, was still lacking the physical confidence that he has today. But Royal Court staff can remember how many fans he won in the intimate surroundings of the 400-seat auditorium, and how many of them stood outside the stage door waiting for an autograph and photo. Not that he was available for dating at that time, as he had only just got back together with his long-term, on-off-and-on-again girlfriend, Olivia Poulet, following a brief separation. The only thing he was available for were auditions, but if only he knew which ones to go for.

Unlike many actors, Benedict seems frequently troubled by his situation, his life and place in society, but he also has the intelligence to articulate his thoughts and the good grace to answer questions carefully. That was certainly the case in 2007 when reporters met him in his dressing room in Sloane Square. They asked him where he was going with his career. He admitted he didn't quite know and he was convinced that it didn't matter. "I know I ought to say my ambition is to take over the world and be the lead in everything, but I'm really happy with the way it is going." Another reporter asked if he felt he was trapped in the theatre. "It's the best place to be," he raved. "I know it sounds wanky, but as an actor, the more I do it, the more I need to do it. It's very painful but you have to do it. It's very nourishing to be on stage, I get a hell of a kick out of it. I'm just ambitious for the work to be good. I don't have a strategy." He did, however, live in the real world. However posh he appeared, he was still just a self-employed, ex-scholarship boy and the son of jobbing actors. "I love theatre, but it doesn't pay the bills," he once said.

What did pay the bills were his next two TV roles. After appearing in so many period dramas and classic plays, he was over the moon to be able get his teeth into something more contemporary. The first of the new roles was in *Stuart: A Life Backwards*, a new BBC drama in which he would play an author taking a backwards glance at his homeless friend Stuart's life. (Benedict has since demonstrated his concern with issues such as homelessness through his long-standing support of The Prince's Trust.)

At the outset, *Stuart: A Life Backwards* looked like it was going to be another tough sell in the same league as *Hawking*. Once again, it was a true story and this time based on the Alexander Masters biography of Stuart Clive Shorter, a homeless man living on the streets of Cambridge in the year 2000. As the title suggests, it takes the unusual approach of detailing Stuart's life from his adult life down through to his childhood, taking in the many contradictions – he was an addict, career criminal, advocate, homeless man, violent psychopath, campaigner, disabled man and victim of sexual abuse – that made him the man he was.

It was while Benedict was on the set of the *Atonement* film that he received a call to gauge his interest in the project. Was he interested? Yes, he was. The book had been so successful that it was only a matter of time before it was turned into a film. It was the kind of biography feature that leant full tilt towards quirkiness with amusing and occasionally disturbing animated moments, mixed in with the downright acerbic. Tom Hardy was cast as Stuart, and according to most critics was an absolute powerhouse, a beguiling mix of the hilarious and the positively frightening, but above all, utterly humane and believable. What made the film work was that it never shied away from the unpalatable aspects of Stuart's life, such as his criminal behaviour and violent outbursts, but Hardy, shouted reviewers, "never alienates or loses the support of the viewer which is an uncanny trick. Like a modern-day, downtrodden, real-life Dickensian character, Stuart was the hero of his own life, and Hardy was able to bring him to life beautifully."

Although Benedict had the far less showy role, he conveyed his character "with a solidity and depth that makes him equally arresting, albeit in a quieter underplayed manner." His journey from disinterested, wryly amused charity worker, who only took the job because of the shift patterns, to compassionate, socially aware man, and above all, a friend to Stuart, is very satisfying. The general consensus was that the film was dramatic, affecting, heartbreaking, offbeat, chilling and often funny. Overall, it was deemed a commendable adaptation and a fitting tribute.

Even so, the difficulty of injecting warmth into a tale of drug abuse, homelessness and violence called for some creative production techniques. The story of a self-harming heroin addict who has suffered terrible sexual abuse seems a particularly bleak subject for a TV project, but Neal Street Productions fought hard to land rights to the critically acclaimed memoir from first-time author Alexander Masters, feeling the story deserved to be told. "It is very dark in places and punctuated by extreme violence," explains producer Pippa Harris. "But there are humorous moments and a central relationship of great warmth, so the cumulative effect is very powerful." As Harris points out, "Stuart is a small-scale story essentially about the friendship between two mismatched individuals which is very harrowing to watch at times." She was making reference to the scenes of sexual abuse. "That would have been hard to sell into a multiplex but it's exceptionally well suited to TV."

Stuart Shorter is a homeless alcoholic who strikes up an unlikely friendship with charity worker Masters. Alexander is intrigued by Stuart's life and traumatic background, and asks him if he can write his story. Stuart agrees but advises him to make the story more exciting by telling it backwards, like a Tom Clancy murder mystery. "We weren't interested in pursuing a story about homelessness," Harris continues. "There are many films which have done that. We felt very strongly that Stuart lived an exceptional life, more interesting than many celebrities or politicians who usually receive biopics, so we wanted to redress that balance."

BBC drama controller Jane Tranter was of the same view and handed creative development to BBC Wales drama chief, Julie Gardner. Despite the fact that Masters had no knowledge of even basic screenplay conventions, Gardner trusted Neal Street's instinct that he was the best person to shape the script. "After the first draft, we made some suggestions and he wrote a very accomplished piece," Harris admits. Till then, Neal Street's focus had been on theatrical features such as *Starter for Ten* and *Revolutionary Road* (starring Leonardo DiCaprio and directed by company co-founder Sam Mendes), but when Masters's literary agent approached them, Harris and co-executive producer Tara Cook were drawn in by the material.

Masters interviewed all those interested in a screen adaptation, but probably chose Neal Street, Harris believes, because its intentions were in tune with his own – to preserve the anarchic character of the book. Masters's pen-and-ink illustrations were replicated as mini-animations within the live action as a way of revealing the author's inner thoughts. "We needed to get the animation to emerge from the live action and merge back into the drama, so we had to be able to provide the animators with fairly detailed shots to work with early on."

Masters worked with design company Knifedge to create 10 animated vignettes. For director David Attwood (Benedict's old ally from *To the Ends of the Earth*), the animations and multiple flashbacks and flash forwards were all part of a process that tasked the audience with solving the puzzle of Stuart's life. "The animations were a visual shorthand for depicting some of the drama in his life without having to laboriously shoot it, as well as enhancing the buddy nature of his relationship with Alexander. What interested me was trying to answer the question of what made him who he was and along the way you come up with lots of different answers."

The actors spent time with homeless groups in Cambridge, along with Masters himself and Shorter's family. Stuart had died in 2002 (before the book was published), so Hardy relied on friends' recollections of him as well as a short BBC2 documentary *Private Investigation* (1999) about the homeless, which Stuart had presented. Shorter suffered from the degenerative disease muscular dystrophy, so part of Hardy's challenge was to capture his stiff movements and peculiar wheezing voice. According to Attwood, Benedict arguably had the harder role since there were fewer obvious traits to build the character around. "If you engage with the actors, you engage with the film. We intentionally shot fairly wide and standing back from the characters with few TV-style close-ups so as not to push the audience towards one answer or another."

Some of the scenes – such as those featuring self-harm – were so disturbing that Attwood shot with two 16mm cameras so Hardy wouldn't have to rehearse multiple takes. "I sometimes didn't tell the actors where the cameras were pointing to give them as much freedom as possible," Attwood admits. "We improvised for longer than usual to bring out their relationship." Attwood stresses that the piece is not meant to be a campaigning piece. "The worse epithet you could level at it is that it's gritty," he says. "The book's tone is not patronizing or worthy but sunny and acerbic, and that's the tone we needed. It's a detailed look at someone's life that asks how honest can we be with ourselves."

After *Stuart*, Benedict's next role would be as gripping as the last had been emotional. Once again he was taking a break from toffs, stately homes, foppish villains or drawing-room dramas, and was swapping period drama for something futuristic. The actor who had not made the cut in a James Bond video game was now going to have a crack at the genre in a thriller about a man whose search for the truth about his brother's death catapults him into an international conspiracy and a passionate love affair.

Filming *The Last Enemy* for the BBC delivered everything Benedict expected from the piece. It was just his second contemporary drama and was, he explains, a riveting story set around the poignant issues of state control and personal liberty, about unique people in a unique situation sparking off a massive political thriller. "I spent every day either running for my life, getting beaten up or making love to my brother's widow," he told *Indie London* when filming had finished. "It was non-stop-dodging bombs from an assassin, being accosted on the street as a homeless person, living in a filthy underground car park, running down corridors or having politicians ruin my life."

Benedict played Stephen Ezard, who reluctantly returns to England from his research lab in China for the funeral of his brother Michael, played by Max Beesley. "We meet Stephen when his personality disorders are at an all-time high," said Benedict. "He is forced out of his hermetically sealed environment on to an aeroplane for Heathrow, thrown back into the force field of his family and literally into another world. He's not your average hero and gets embroiled in a story which is all out of his control, which is hard for someone who has such a controlling personality."

He continues, "Stephen's turmoil begins when he meets Michael's wife Yasim after the funeral. He intended to return to China but he falls in love with this extraordinary woman who is his brother's widow. Then he is asked to get involved in a government project. He finds it hard to confront any of the decisions or conflicts that come up. Initially, he is apathetic. He doesn't know who to trust, or who is deceiving him but instead of letting events overtake him he is forced to become proactive."

As usual, Benedict spent quite some time preparing to play the role. "Stephen is an incredibly bright but isolated soul. When he is working as a scientist, it's almost like he is reading Braille. There's something very artistic about it, like he's conducted it because he's highly capable of making connections and seeing patterns in the illogical. That's why his work is attractive to the government. I researched hypochondria and obsessive-compulsive disorder and found the surgeon's style of hand washing and adapted that to Stephen so it would be an intense and thorough ritual. I came up with the idea that his mother was a skilled violinist and Stephen has a dexterity, which showed as a physical tic to externalize his thought process. It was great fun to create a story but it has to be done subtly." In the end, adds Benedict, "I really ended up liking him. He is eccentric but if people suspend their judgement they will see a lot of themselves in him – all the things we don't want to confront, not always enjoying social situations or interacting with others well."

What Benedict liked most of all, was how Stephen changes dramatically as the drama unfolds. "At the beginning he is neutral and anonymous. The only colour about him is his hair and eyes. He's quite athletic and eats healthily but his trench coat covers up his frame. As time goes on, he gets more and more bedraggled from being beaten and bruised. He becomes more streetwise and learns how to hold a gun. He also becomes much more open and loose, physically he is still guarded but he has mellowed. He has flown out of his shell into this massive love affair and is blown away by it." All the same, Benedict admits that he felt more at home with the Stephen of later episodes. "Tapping a computer screen is not my thing and I had to learn to type and talk at the same time which was quite tricky. I prefer to be an action hero, not the geek by the screen. It was great fun to learn a bit of stunt driving and flying through the air with explosions behind me going off all over the place!"

Working with his co-stars was equally rewarding. "Anamaria [Marinca] was a fine performer and she's incredibly professional. Filming in Bucharest was extraordinarily hot. We had 5,000 watts burning into a small set and it took all your will and strength and concentration. We both had to overcome the difficulty of the love scenes, especially as English is not her first language. Max was a joy to work with as well. We are chalk and cheese in real life but we became very close. He has great energy and enthusiasm and is a real gent, as is Robert Carlyle. He is cracking as Russell and was so involved and trusting. It was a huge operation but the director kept everyone's spirits up. He had manic energy, puppyish enthusiasm and great overall vision."

It seemed only natural that, after proving he could hold his own in any company with significant roles, Benedict would continue in the same vein. His next project therefore came as something of a surprise. The actor would be playing William Carey, Mary Boleyn's husband, in a romanticized account of the one-time mistress of King Henry VIII, and her sister, Anne, who of course became the monarch's ill-fated second wife. However, Benedict had his reasons for taking on such a small role. The film had a £35 million budget, he would have the chance to work alongside some of his favourite actor buddies, and last but not least, he would be kissing Scarlett Johansson! Back home, he defied any of his friends to pass up on such an opportunity.

Adapted from Philippa Gregory's bestselling novel, *The Other Boleyn Girl* follows the fierce rivalry between sisters Mary and Anne Boleyn (played by Natalie Portman and Scarlett Johansson) as – under pressure from their father and uncle – they compete to win the affections of Eric Bana's Tudor King Henry VIII. The Boleyn family is desperate to promote its position in society, and what better way to rise through the ranks than for one of the sisters to secure the royal prize. But life in Henry's court is very different to the rural life that the two women are accustomed to, and before long their close relationship has become one of bitter rivalry.

In the days after the *Boleyn* shoot, Benedict, once again, went through some serious bouts of soul-searching about his career. Away from the spotlight, he had managed to carve out a useful niche in radio drama. His voice, distinctive, yet adaptable, was perfect for all sorts of productions. He was on air in a host of different shows. Over the years, they had included a one-off version of everything from *Doctor Who* to *Blake's 7*. Benedict also won a part alongside Stephanie Cole in the long-running airline comedy *Cabin Pressure* and he became the definitive "Young Rumpole" in the latest offshoot of the *Rumpole of the Bailey* series.

Despite a cameo in the controversial British film *Four Lions* directed by Chris Morris, Benedict knew that the roles he played on television, in film and on stage were far less varied than the ones he enjoyed on radio, which in turn would have him thinking about how best to choose his next gig. Part of him listened to people who said he was in danger of being typecast, part of him listened to hard-up drama school colleagues who said being typecast was better than being unemployed, and part of him felt he would be content being a big name in the relatively small world of London theatre. However, another part of him was finally ready to test himself against the best on Broadway or in Hollywood.

Each different voice needed to be heard, even when his agent told him he had been approached to play the lead in a National Theatre production of Terence Rattigan's *After the Dance*. He ended up accepting the role of David Scott-Fowler, simply because he considered it to be a dream part for most actors, and of course, because he loved theatre, but that didn't stop him hesitating before taking up the offer. To many, the play's depiction of bright young things in the interwar twenties, whirling towards doom in a haze of cocktail parties, seemed a little too brittle and too clipped. Was the part of Scott-Fowler, the rich, alcoholic monster of charm at its centre, too easy in terms of class for Benedict, who has still fighting against typecasting? Was it time for Benedict to break free of such posh characters and their gilded drawing rooms?

After the Dance portrays a young, fashionable set getting older but still drinking and partying as the nation slides to war. The original production opened in June 1939 to good reviews but closed early as the country's mood changed, and it has been staged only rarely since. However, as it was Rattigan's centenary year and there were revivals of his plays across the country, *After the Dance* seemed a good choice for the National. But according to the play's director, Thea Sharrock, it had not been easy to get such a little-known play staged. The National's Nicholas Hytner, best known for directing the much acclaimed screen adaptation of

Arthur Miller's *The Crucible* with Daniel Day-Lewis and Winona Ryder, was reluctant and initially declined. "He said: 'No, I don't think so, but let's try and find something else.'" But then, Hytner changed his mind after re-reading the play. "At which point, " says Sharrock, "I got really nervous and said: 'Can I go away and think about it?' And by hook or by crook it happened."

Certainly, Sharrock was one of the factors that eventually lured Benedict into accepting the role. He read *After the Dance* again, and it got under his skin. "There is an instant music to it, but lots going on underneath. It was a time of repression, and the emotional impact of Rattigan's plays lies in what he reserves and eventually lets go. All the nuances that you sometimes mine hard for in vain with other writers are there." It also helped that he had gone to Rattigan's old school, Harrow, had lived in the same house as he did and was in the Ratt Society drama group. And let's not forget that his "first big, silly role," as he calls it was in Rattigan's *The Browning Version*. All in all, it was a bit of everything that made him right for the role of David, and made him think that he would like more of a challenge. But he also saw the part as an actor's gift.

"David Scott-Fowler is a witty Lord of Misrule, fatally attractive to women, who destroys everything around him. The childish purity of his selfishness is hard to take but I have to like the character because people seem to fall in love with him," Benedict explained to Nick Curtis of the *London Evening Standard*. "I have to make him likeable in order for him not to be hateable." Even if he was wary of making too strong a case for the play's contemporary relevance, he also saw something in the play that others might initially be unaware of, a parallel with the imminence of the Second World War for the bright young things that may accord with the prevalent sense of uncertainty in our own time. He was also aware that a mixed elite of the privileged, the monied and the brilliant is still with us, including the self-destructive elements like "your Amy Winehouses or Pete Dohertys." As Curtis put it in his article, Benedict was appearing in a class-bound play at a time when class and privilege, as manifested by the leaders of the coalition government, were back on the agenda. He even asked Benedict if it was easier to come out as a private school-educated posh boy now? "Christ, no!" Benedict snapped. "I think you have to hide it more with Cameron in charge. Class has always been with us, it just moves into different areas. In Rattigan's day it was incredibly stratified. What's interesting now is how far class will be defined by money, what the tax rises and the income thresholds and the VAT increases will be." Was he hoping that the then current instability at home and abroad would result in a more egalitarian society? Perhaps he was. On a professional level at least, it nagged him that, in the UK, he's allowed to play above his social class but not below it, "whereas in America I could play everything from trailer-trash to Harvard-educated."

On top of the lure of working with a talented director, it was also a family feeling that swayed Benedict's final decision. He remembered the times his parents had brought him to the National Theatre as a child. He remembered the buzz they had always felt afterwards. He wanted to give them that buzz again, this was their son up on the big stage. The plan worked. Benedict remembers that his dad, in particular, was moved to tears after the first night. "He was telling me how proud he was. I didn't know what to do. I just held onto him. I said: You're not crying out of relief that I got through it, are you? And he said: No, you stupid boy. I'm crying because you were so wonderful."

What no one knew was that this kind of acclaim was about to become commonplace. All the soul-searching and the careful choosing of roles had been worthwhile. The months and years of learning his craft in small theatres and on low-budget TV was about to pay off. In the summer of 2010, Benedict was about to hit the jackpot. The posh boy from all those old plays was about to go mainstream. The world was about to meet a very new Sherlock Holmes – but before that, he had to finish treading the boards at the National Theatre in *After the Dance* and promote his latest on-screen role in D R Hood's *Wreckers*. The film was premiered at the London Film Festival with a Q&A appearance at the Curzon Cinema in Soho, not long after Benedict's appearance in Hattie Dalton's *Third Star* had closed the Edinburgh International Film Festival that same summer.

Benedict's roles in both films have since proven characteristic of his favourite kind of role and are the sort of material he seems to relish getting his teeth into. In *Wreckers* he plays David, a teacher, who has set up home with his new wife, Dawn, in the small town where he grew up. However, the facade of the couple's superficially tranquil life is soon put to the test with the arrival of David's brother Nick, who threatens to drive a wedge between the newlyweds when he challenges Dawn's perception of her husband.

However, it was *Third Star* that offered Benedict the more challenging role. Terminally ill with cancer, his character summons three of his closest friends for a life-changing final trip together with the intention of setting their lives straight. However his friends also have some things they would like to get off their chests and the film twists into something funnier and more unpredictable than a simple plot summary might suggest. "I think it explores sides of friendship that are often neglected," says Benedict. "The streaks of competitiveness, support, love, irritation and trust are all here. But I also liked the idea that being robbed of your life too early doesn't give you the right to tell others how to live."

As usual, Benedict carried out detailed research in order to fully understand his character, meeting members of the Sarcoma Society. However, the movie also had personal resonances for him, because Dr Roger Poulet, father of his girlfriend Olivia, had been given a terminal diagnosis four years earlier. "It was a remarkable thing," says Benedict. "I was someone to whom he could speak and be emotionally very open to without fear of upsetting his family. He didn't want to atone and he had no fears about what he'd left behind for his family, but he would talk about wanting people to understand him. So along with Olivia and her brother James, he composed this extraordinary *Desert Island Discs* memorial for himself. Listening to it after the funeral, hearing his voice again and laughing at his jokes was utterly odd and profound. He managed to create this extraordinary memory of himself that was utterly true to who he was. And literally, we had just buried Olivia's father when the script for *Third Star* arrived, so I completely connected with it as soon as I read it."

Chapter 6
"A Study in Pink"

It all started three years earlier on a train to Wales. Writers Mark Gatiss and Steven Moffat were on their way to the *Doctor Who* set at the BBC's production centre in Cardiff. Their discussions usually focused on the *Doctor Who* episodes they were working on, but often they talked about their love and obsession for Sherlock Holmes, wondering how they could resurrect the famous detective for primetime TV without making it look like a remake of the Basil Rathbone movies they both adored.

The more they kicked their thoughts around, the more they liked the idea. In the end, they decided they could take Conan Doyle's creation and drag him into the twenty-first century, kicking and screaming if necessary. They loved the idea of seeing their iconic hero in modern-day London. They saw nicotine patches instead of an ancient pipe. They saw GPS systems instead of a magnifying glass, and they wanted blogs to be written instead of journals. They thought a total re-working of the classic stories could work. And they weren't alone.

The powers-that-be at the BBC were quick to offer a development deal when the concept was pitched to them. Initial scripts were written and a pilot episode was planned. The budget if it all came off, would be substantial. The aim was to produce a primetime hit that could be sold around the world. But would it really work? The team knew success or failure would all hinge on one key detail. Everything would depend on them finding the perfect Sherlock Holmes.

With so much at stake, you would imagine a lot of time was set aside for the audition and selection process. You would imagine that dozens, or possibly, hundreds of actors would have been seen and auditioned. And you would think there would be repeat call-backs, detailed screen tests – even a focus group or two on the casting. You would be wrong. The search ended the moment the team auditioned Benedict. "He was the only person we offered Sherlock to," says Gatiss.

The pair knew who he was and they knew what he could do, and they were prepared to take a risk on him. He was always a weird elder brother or the rapist, was Moffat's take on Benedict's career at that time. But the moment he met him, he was certain he had found his offbeat oddball of a leading man. "He does have the look, he's got that imperious style and he's a bit Byronic." From that moment, Gatiss and Moffat were convinced that Benedict was also one of the few actors around who could play "a show-off, self-obsessed egotist and yet still be loved." Funnily enough, it was more or less the same reason why David Attwood had cast him in

To the Ends of the Earth five years earlier. Benedict had the knack of playing intensely dislikeable characters, and ending up deeply liked. Not so easy was casting the perfect Dr Watson, not least because the chemistry between the two leads had to work from the start. The production team considered a whole host of capable actors. Then, they selected the man who has made that role his own. Martin Freeman, five years Benedict's senior, would play a very modern soldier just back from Afghanistan in a clear echo of the earlier Afghan war when Conan Doyle's books were set.

Martin was the youngest of five children born to Geoff Freeman and Philomena R Norris. His grandfather was a member of the Royal Army Medical Corps during the evacuation of Dunkirk in 1940, who was killed in a bombing raid two days before his unit was able to leave. Martin attended Salesian School, a Roman Catholic comprehensive school in Surrey, followed by the Central School of Speech and Drama in London. From 1997, he appeared in small roles across theatre, film and television, including *The Bill* and *Casualty* before landing his biggest and most recognizable role as Tim Canterbury in *The Office* in 2001, alongside Ricky Gervais. Two years later, Martin gained the lead role in the beloved ITV sitcom *Hardware*, set in a DIY shop, and then, in the same year, he was part of the ensemble cast of the all-star Richard Curtis romantic comedy *Love, Actually*. He was BAFTA-nominated in 2004 for his performance in *The Office Christmas Special* and one year after that, played Arthur Dent in the big screen adaptation of Douglas Adams's *The Hitchhiker's Guide to the Galaxy*, perhaps his single most prominent role up to that time. A variety of cameos followed in films as well as roles in a various short films, continuing until 2009 when he was cast as John Watson. He is probably best known today for his starring role in Peter Jackson's *The Hobbit*, which followed his success in *Sherlock*. Away from the screen, and away from the *Sherlock* set, Martin and Benedict would become good friends despite being total opposites.

With other key roles cast, the script finalized and shooting schedules arranged, it looked as if it was all systems go. Everyone gave their all when the pilot episode was filmed. Belief in the project was total and everyone was desperate for it to succeed. But it seemed as if they could all be in for a big disappointment. When the pilot was shown to the BBC executives and programme schedulers, they sat stony-faced in the screening rooms. They didn't get the magic that everyone else had experienced on set and they didn't like it. Many of the executives went one step further – they hated it. It could have been killed off there and then, but Gatiss, Moffat and the show's other big wigs were determined to change the executives' minds. They tried everything to persuade them that the show would work, but it seemed a stalemate had been reached. More meetings were held and more solutions discussed. In London, the writers, producers, paymasters and schedulers all pitched in with their different points of view. In Wales, and scattered around the rest of the country, the cast and crew crossed their fingers and hoped for the best. Insiders agreed that there had been a really strong sense of excitement about the project. The team was devastated to hear rumours that it had all been for nothing. Benedict felt particularly vulnerable. This was supposed to be his

Above: Benedict's actor-parents, Timothy Carlton and Wanda Ventham as they were seen in an episode of ITV's *Crown Court* in 1977, one year after Benedict was born.

Below: The earliest known photo of Benedict at just three days old with his proud parents at the Queen Charlotte's Hospital in West London, July 1976.

One of Benedict's earliest television roles in *Fortysomething*. He is shown here with co-stars Neil Henry, Emma Ferguson and Siobhan Hewlett.

Benedict made his big screen debut in *Starter for Ten* in which he shared most of his scenes with Alice Eve, James McAvoy, Mark Gatiss and Elaine Tan. He would, years later, reunite with both Eve for *Star Trek Into Darkness* and with Gatiss on BBC's *Sherlock*.

Opposite, above: On stage in *The Arsonists* at the Royal Court Theatre, London, November 2007. One of Benedict's favourite theatres where his father had appeared 40 years before. He is pictured here with his fellow cast members, Will Keen, Zawe Ashton, Jacqueline Defferary and Paul Chahidi.

Opposite, below: In 2008, Benedict became the envy of his friends when he shared an on-screen kiss with Scarlet Johansson in *The Other Boleyn Girl,* and got the chance to work alongside Eddie Redmayne, Natalie Portman and Jim Sturgess.

Right: Benedict with his girlfriend Olivia Poulet whom he dated for 12 years after meeting her at Manchester University.

Above: Benedict with co-star Martin Freeman on the London set of *The Empty Hearse,* the first episode of series 3 of *Sherlock.* It became the most anticipated, watched and talked about show of the entire series.

Opposite: Benedict as David Scott-Fowler and Nancy Carroll as his wife Joan, in the 2010 revival of Terence Rattigan's much neglected play, *After The Dance* at the Lyttelton Theatre in London.

Next page: Benedict as Sherlock Holmes, the role that turned him into a household name and made him the most popular actor on British television.

big break. It was a primetime starring role on national television, and now it looked as if no one would ever see it. And he might never get this close to the big time again.

Luckily for everyone, a compromise was reached and experts say it was worth waiting for. Having pulled the show back from the brink, the BBC decided to ditch the pilot show altogether. It gave the green light for three complete 90-minute episodes. The first was a complete re-shoot of the troubled pilot. It was heavily rewritten, remoulded and refocused. Over a year later, when the pilot was released as a surprise extra on the series one DVD, media expert Mark Lawson analyzed it and came to a fascinating conclusion. "Media studies courses should clear space on the syllabus for a remarkable illustration of the differences that creative rethinking and editorial intervention can make," he wrote in the *Guardian*. "Both the pilot and the transmitted opening episode are called "A Study in Pink", have the same plot line (a spate of suicides in London) and an almost identical cast. The second version, though, has been substantially expanded and rewritten, and completely re-imagined in look, pace and sound. Most notably, the scene that made me think when watching a preview that the series might be something special – a blizzard of insolent text messages from Sherlock appearing on the screen during Lestrade's press conference – is missing from the pilot, as is a crucial sub-plot involving a confusion between Moriarty and Mycroft. The overall impact of the changes is to achieve the paradox for which crime fiction aims: making the story clearer in some ways but more mysterious in others. In the remake, we see more of the suicides, while the striking device of the text and email printouts on screen gives Benedict's Holmes a looming, almost supernatural presence before he is formally introduced. Watching both versions side by side, viewers in effect eavesdrop on feedback and script-notes discussions, gaining an unusual entry to the nicotine-patch-filled rooms where television drama is made. What's fascinating is that the trial programme led to BBC and media rumours that Sherlock was a potential disaster. When the glossy, confident, witty series was eventually shown, it seemed the gossip must have been wrong. But, as it turns out, it wasn't."

Filming of that second version, and of the two other episodes, began in and around Cardiff's *Doctor Who* studios in early 2009. That made Benedict smile, because he had already considered himself for the part of the Doctor after David Tennant was known to be leaving the role, and before Matt Smith was cast as the eleventh incarnation. According to insiders, Benedict had even spoken to David about the role, but decided not to pursue it, because says Benedict, "I thought it would have to be radically different. And anyway, I didn't really like the whole package, being on school lunch boxes." As far as Benedict was concerned it was out of the question. Even after Smith's departure had been announced, and he again became the hot favourite, the rumours that he was about to become the twelfth Doctor were wildly exaggerated.

But he was also smiling because he knew that the new Holmes would be on screen in competition with the new *Zen* detective mysteries starring Rufus Sewell, and Kenneth Branagh's portrayal of the Scandinavian detective *Wallander*. "Rufus, who's a mate of mine, gets Italy in spring, Ken Branagh gets Sweden in summer, and I get Cardiff and Newport in January and February." According to insiders, it became one of Benedict's standard jokes, among friends, but sometimes, on set, the joke wore a little thin. Some say it was so cold he had to hold hot water bottles to his cheeks to warm up his jaw for his latest rush of quick-fire words.

All the same, everyone on the set agreed that Benedict did bring something special to the role, and that playing Sherlock as he did wasn't as easy as it looked. What the Sherlock creators had produced had to tread a very fine line. He would be very easy to dislike, so Benedict had to do something clever to keep audiences on side. Then, of course, there was the densely written script.

Those rapid-fire deduction scenes involve whole walls of words, all to be delivered at top speed by an actor at the top of his game. Sometimes it was the verbal equivalent of all the scientific formulae he had to chalk up on the blackboards in *Hawking* back at the start of his television career. You couldn't just glance at your scripts the night before and hope to wing it on acting autopilot. Benedict had to do his homework as usual. He had to immerse himself in the role. And, once again it took its toll on his body. He kept on working when he thought he had a case of flu halfway through filming. He kept on swimming, doing Bikram yoga and taking a daily dose of honey to try and stay in shape, but even he couldn't fight this one off. When his temperature hit 39.4°C, it was clear he had pneumonia. While some said he should have been hospitalized, Benedict was determined to stay on set. He knew that it would cost a fortune to shut down production, even for a matter of days.

So he shut his body down for the few days he wasn't on set. He forced himself to rest and regain his strength. If he looked a little paler and more angular when he returned to work, then all the better. His modern-day Sherlock wasn't the picture of health at the best of times.

The other thing Benedict could do on his rare time off was terrify himself about the way his portrayal of Sherlock Holmes might be received – Conan Doyle fans are a loyal and demanding bunch. As expected, plenty of letters and emails came flooding in, and there was also a great deal of Internet chatter that told him what people thought. "We're setting out to do something new and they have let me know that I have huge shoes to fill." Despite all the off-set dramas, the production that came together on the screen looked amazing. The interaction between Benedict and Martin, Sherlock and his Watson, was particularly strong. It was the start of a true romance, totally modern, full of humour and utterly believable.

But what would TV viewers make of it all? Would it be a hit or a career-ending flop? Benedict and the rest of the cast had to sit tight for a long time before finding out. The first episode didn't air until 25 July 2010, and when it came, Benedict was in for something of a shock. The big time looked set to arrive at last. He was going to be in the eye of his first real media storm.

The BBC publicity department was pulling out all the stops to make sure *Sherlock* was a hit, which meant putting Benedict in front of as many cameras and reporters as possible. It was something Benedict wasn't particularly comfortable or keen about. No photo shoots were going to be easy for a man who jokes he's got a weird-shaped head and looks like Sid the Sloth from *Ice Age*. The interviews could be just as awkward. One of the reporters from the *Guardian* newspaper remembers how ill at ease Benedict seemed to be with the whole situation. "He twists in his chair. He sits on his hands. He does impromptu imitations and funny voices and his eyes jag from side to side." Other reports confirmed that Benedict needed two coffees, five cigarettes, quite a bit of water and some juice before he could face the press. To make matters worse, several chat-show producers joked they needed a steady-cam to film a man who never seemed to be still. One problem with the whole public relations gig was that the self-effacing, terminally self-deprecating Benedict hadn't been brought up to brag. He could hog the limelight on stage and he could dominate a room when he was playing a part, but he wasn't great when it came to talking about himself.

Other commentators noted that he was entirely natural. "Until now, Cumberbatch has never been a household face. He has had small parts in big films and big parts in small films." Now, of course, he had the biggest part of what could be the biggest show on Earth. Moffat predicted that Benedict could become "one of the hottest young actors on the planet." It was a far, far cry from the art-house theatres where he had previously been little more than a big fish in a small and rarefied pond. Moffat's prediction came true. *Sherlock* the show was a triumph and its lead was a sensation.

The traditional critics adored everything about the show and four- and five-star reviews dominated the papers and TV magazines.

If anything, the online critics were just as impressed, and in the age of the Internet, these fans could be even more important. Chat rooms, message boards and fan sites exploded with interest. Facebook and Twitter were awash with recommendations and positive comments. In a media world where everyone seemed to be dumbing down, Benedict was applauded for making it cool to be brainy. He was lauded for his command of language and he was even being lusted after, which triggered a burst of very salacious fan fiction from an army of self-styled "Cumberbitches". By the time the short three-episode series ended, it was clear that Benedict's life would never be the same again. No more would he tramp unnoticed across his beloved Hampstead Heath in north London, and never again could he be entirely anonymous when he stopped at red traffic lights on his pushbike or his Honda CBF600 motorbike. Indeed, the days when he could waste a pleasant, unobtrusive hour in a Soho coffee shop or in his other favourite haunt, the fifth floor café of the Waterstones book shop on London's Piccadilly, were over.

All the same, Benedict was enjoying the changes fame had brought him. He wasn't going to turn into one of those people who dream of stardom for so long, only to claim they hate it when it arrives. By contrast, Benedict continued to embrace his newfound fame as *The Sunday Times* reporter remembers when they met that extraordinary summer. "He seems wired with the excitement of it all, rewarded for his abundant charm with the goodwill of everyone he meets, from waitresses, dogs, his co-stars to the ancient eccentric with the pipe on Hampstead Heath who stands next to him for a photograph, and my smitten seven-year-old who is in the back of the car when we drive to another café."

A short while later, Benedict found that his fame was spreading. At home, rankings for *Sherlock* rose for each of the three shows. They hit nine million by the end of the too short run – in the height of summer when most people are either on holiday or in the garden. Television insiders said that a score of five million viewers would have been a success for *Sherlock*. Winning almost twice as many was a triumph. Better still, it wasn't a one-off. *Sherlock* was broadcast on the PBS art channel in America. Sure, it was never going to rival something like *American Idol* on a channel like Fox, but ratings were still well ahead of trend for the channel. The reviews and audience feedback were second to none. Even the online community in America warmed to this oddball Brit. It would come as no surprise that the rest of the world now demanded a share in the fun of it all. Needless to say, the show would go on to be sold to an incredible 180 countries, making a fortune for the BBC and guaranteeing a second series almost as soon as the scripts could be written.

But before the cast could be summoned back to Wales, Benedict had lined up another headline-grabbing job. He was staying in London for a while and was heading south of the River Thames to take on another leading role at the National Theatre. And this time, things were going to get bloody.

Chapter 7

Frankenstein

When Danny Boyle, the director of the Oscar-winning *Slumdog Millionaire* announced he was directing a unique version of *Frankenstein* for the National Theatre, he promised his production would be grim, gritty and like nothing anyone had seen before. Based on Mary Shelley's famous Gothic novel that has spawned countless movies since the 1930s and introduced Boris Karloff as the monster with bolts through his neck, the new stage adaptation would also have a twist. Boyle didn't want one actor to play Victor Frankenstein every night while another played his monster. He wanted two actors to play both roles, alternating every night so audiences would never know who or what to expect. But first he needed to find two actors to carry it off. Those two actors turned out to be Benedict and Jonny Lee Miller.

As Boyle explains, "I always wanted to do it with two actors. I always thought it was an amazing way to explore the story. What better way to put the focus on the fact that they are one in a way, that they're the same person really? I thought how can we find a couple of actors who will do that? I knew Jonny, I had worked with him once before but I'd never worked with Benedict... I thought that's interesting, I know him and I don't know him, and that will be interesting as well, and that's what we tried to do throughout, and that's what we tried to explore."

Although Boyle had worked with Miller previously (when Miller had played Sick Boy in Boyle's 1996 *Trainspotting*), the pair had not been in touch since then. In fact, since shooting to fame in Boyle's movie, Miller's career had been chequered to say the least. It's had plenty of ups and downs. The downs have included films that never saw the light of day and television series that were unexpectedly pulled. The ups were a successful run alongside Sienna Miller on Broadway in *After Miss Julie*, a turn in Peter Travis's critically acclaimed *Endgame*, and since 2012, quite ironically, he has been playing Benedict's role of Sherlock Holmes in *Elementary*, the US update of the Holmes stories. Today, Miller exudes quiet contentment with his lot though. But he admits that, as he progresses through his 30s, work is harder to come by, and for six months the year before *Frankenstein*, there was nothing at all. Looking back on *Trainspotting* and everything that happened since, he has no regrets. Even though he lived out every man's (and perhaps woman's) dream of briefly being married to Angelina Jolie, as far as work went, Miller admits, he didn't really capitalize on it in the correct way.

Boyle, however, didn't really know Benedict as a stage actor. "I knew what a fine screen actor he was, but there's a physicality involved in the theatre. It's not just about mannerisms or impersonation, which screen often is, it's about sustaining a narrative with mind and body. When I saw him for *Frankenstein*, that was the only thing I wanted to know. Did he have that physical capacity? We met and I asked him to do a few things and he was extraordinary in the room. He's as fit as a boxer, which you have to be for the stage. You have to have an internal fitness that allows you to carry the story so it never sags. He had this combination of the cerebral and the physical, which you can see when you look back at his screen work in *Hawking*, it's there. *Frankenstein* was a great one for using it."

Boyle learned a great deal from working with Benedict. He was most impressed, though, with how he took the dual role very much in his stride. Nothing seemed to faze him. "Any part when you're exposed on the stage is a challenge," Boyle expounded. "You put yourself on the line, but doing that twice and seeing yourself through someone else's eyes is a credit to his confidence levels. He was able to take it on. Actors like Benedict are on a trajectory, which is natural, and we haven't laced our way into it yet but we're about to. I think the film world will see that now."

The idea of doing a new stage version of *Frankenstein* had first been discussed with playwright Nick Dear back in the early 1990s, when both Boyle and Dear were working on *The Last Days of Don Juan* for The Royal Shakespeare Company. According to Boyle, Nick's first drafts were pretty close to the novel, but then, "we came up with the idea to start the play from the Creature's point of view, to give the monster its voice back, which had been lost throughout most of its film adaptations." Unlike most of those movie treatments, Boyle and Dear were committed to staging a version of the story that remained true to Shelley's original novel where both Frankenstein and the Creature end up in the wilderness at the end of the story. It was very important, says Boyle, to have Victor and the Creature bond together in death.

It is probably what fascinated them both about the story. But then again, Mary Shelley's *Frankenstein* is still as fascinating as it ever was, and even if it wasn't quite as popular as *Dracula*, it is still one of the most enduring works of Gothic horror and science-fiction literature, and ranks among the best-known novels of English Romanticism. Although most people are in some way familiar with the story through the movies – if not through the Universal Karloff version, then certainly through the host of British-made "Hammer Horror" movies that made household names of Peter Cushing and Christopher Lee – most have no idea that the tale is based on an almost 200-year-old novel and even fewer have read it. In fact, the fame of Victor Frankenstein and his creation is based mainly on various adaptations and rewritings of the original nineteenth-century novel. Like *Dracula* and vampires, the Frankenstein myth entered twentieth-century popular culture and has become part of it in the same way as Coca Cola, James Bond, Levi's Jeans, Mickey Mouse, Elvis Presley and the Beatles. First adaptations of Shelley's novel appeared shortly after its initial publication in the form of plays written for the stage. Since then, Frankenstein and his monster have appeared in countless forms, mostly movies but also in horror and science-fiction novels by various writers, TV programmes and pop songs. Even children's books and cartoons featuring a less scary version of the monster have appeared over the years. So, why risk another retelling for the London stage when the story's been done a hundred times before?

The answer is that no one had done anything like the version that Boyle and Dear were about to let loose on the London theatre community. Certainly that was likely to have been the opinion of some insiders and observers as Boyle, Benedict and Miller worked out how to overcome one of their first hurdles – how best to work together to make everything work on stage as well as it looked on paper.

"One consideration was that they might rehearse separately, unless they were in the same scene," says Boyle. But as Benedict and Miller befriended each other very early on, they didn't really find that to be a useful way to work. "We're not precious," explained Miller. "We find it constructive to talk to each other about what looks good and what doesn't. We're more of a team."

"The dialogue," added Benedict, "between us is selfless and co-operative. If there's something really good that he does, I will ask if I can incorporate it." To many, it sounded like they were stealing ideas from each other; however, as Benedict argued, isn't that what actors do? "There's no shame in stealing, and any actor who says he doesn't is lying. You steal from everything." But not every idea worked. One that was tried out in rehearsals – to have a pool of slime, like amniotic fluid, around the sac where the Creature comes out – looked and worked fantastically, but they had to give up on it because the stage would have been too slippery for actors to perform on.

On another occasion, during their research, Benedict and Miller gruesomely observed an autopsy at St Thomas' Hospital in London, which is normally not possible because anyone who attends an autopsy has to have permission from relatives. However, on this occasion, the autopsy was for a 40-year-old man who had died of a drug overdose and had no known relatives. According to Benedict, it was an extraordinary experience. It's where "I learnt what a dead body looks like when it's open, when the organs are examined and weighed, what the skin looks like when it's cut and peeled back, what the subcutaneous levels look like, what the muscles look like, how hard it is to saw through bone, how much certain organs weigh. It's life, it's all of us. It was fascinating and there was personality in the person on the table but it was like a prosthetic. You couldn't get over that fact. It was like we've all been desensitized by brilliant, brilliant films and brilliant technicians in films because we've been brought so close already to the reality of what it is like to stand in a room watching a dissection, but it was remarkable."

Equally remarkable was first night. Reporters remember meeting a Benedict who was "clutching a bottle of water and a chunk of raw ginger, and apologizing for what he terms a touch of Franko flu." As usual, Benedict was able to fight off his illness just in time for when the play finally opened on 5 February 2011, and just as well. The celebrity-studded first night was a triumph as were the extraordinary reviews that followed.

The London papers loved Benedict and so too did everything from the *New York Times* to the *Hollywood Reporter*, which declared that Benedict was superb in both roles. "Cumberbatch nails Frankenstein's air of innate superiority on one night, and makes heartbreaking the creature's aching search for wisdom and compassion on the next." The end result was that *Frankenstein* was the hottest ticket in town, as were the simultaneous transmissions that were beamed into cinemas around the country. They too, were sell-out events for National Theatre Live, first in the spring of 2011 and through encore broadcasts the following year, and again during the National Theatre's fiftieth-year celebrations in November 2013. The idea was to allow thousands across the UK and the world to watch a show that they might not otherwise have the chance to see.

More importantly, Benedict enthused, "it was very important for the democratization of seeing art in Britain and for there to be an outreach beyond the theatre. The broadcasts were certainly part of what brought the theatre performance to the national consciousness in a way that is rare for the theatre, but it was also the themes of the work that made it stand out. There are massive issues of parenting, of race, of social codes and conduct, of sexual politics – it's just a bit of a feast, really, for whatever issue you want to look at. And it's rip-roaring entertainment. And it's savagely beautiful and funny, and moving, all at the same time. It's quite a total experience."

"The opening 10 minutes were stunning," shouted Henry Hitchings in the *London Evening Standard*. "They are as atmospheric as theatre ever gets. When the naked Creature emerges from a papery womb, he writhes spectacularly. Slowly he adjusts to his surroundings, and his tentative engagement with the world is thrillingly conveyed." Charles Spencer in the *Daily Telegraph* agreed: "At its best, there is no doubt that *Frankenstein* is the most viscerally exciting and visually stunning show in town." Even the *Daily Mail's* Patrick Marmion managed not to take umbrage at all the genitals on display. "Despite all the hype, the show does not disappoint," he enthused. "Boyle directs the gothic classic like a kid in a toy shop." There were, of course, the usual debates over the comparative merits of Benedict and Miller, and which one of them was more fabulous. "It is an astonishing performance… Cumberbatch's Creature is unforgettable," wrote Michael Billington, who is not usually given to such hyperbole. Even Paul Taylor managed to crank his praise for Miller into nineteenth gear: "He takes us further into the feeling," Taylor said, "with a flailing, straining L-plate biped's ballet of spasmodic convulsions and electrocuted sensitivity." There was not one bad review and the general consensus was that *Frankenstein* was a hit.

Not so good was the news that halfway through the three-month run; Benedict was exhausted and battered, and was concerned that his body might never return to normal. "My wrists are turning into ankles, I've joints coming out my fucking hips, I've had problems with my neck, my voice has come and gone, I've had concussions, I've had cuts, I've got a thing in my left foot called *plantar fasciitis*, which means the tendons ball up into a ball of agony. I don't think anyone could do it for too long if they give it the sort of welly we are giving it. There's a limit to us humans. You come off stage and you've just shed five pounds of body weight. It is tough, our bodies are all in pain. It's fascinating, sort of crippling ourselves doing this. I've spent time in X-ray today. We've had all sorts of injuries, it's a hard show to do, but it's also been wonderful."

Miller was feeling exactly the same, and several months down the line, the two co-stars were thrilled to share the Olivier and Evening Standard Award for Best Actor. But before then, they had to make it through to the end of the run. They had to shout and fight and laugh and cry amidst extraordinary pyrotechnics on one of the largest stages in Britain. The plan was to stay healthy, manage their minor injuries and rely on the fact that they could fully relax and put their feet up once the limited run ended, or rather that was the plan. Not that it quite worked out like that. One week after the final curtain call, Benedict would be heading off to Dartmoor to start filming the most famous of all Sherlock Holmes stories. And he was also about to get a call from Steven Spielberg.

Chapter 8

From Baker Street to Middle Earth

When Steven Spielberg went to see *War Horse* on stage at the National Theatre in London, he was so blown away by it that he wanted to turn the tale into a movie. After optioning the film rights, he started the casting process; one of the first calls he made was to Benedict's agent, who in turn called Benedict and told him that Spielberg was a fan of his work, had loved the first series of *Sherlock* and was completely moved by his performance in *Frankenstein*. And oh yes, he wanted him to read a script and then go and meet him.

That meeting, however, almost didn't happen. A couple of hours before the curtain was set to rise on *Frankenstein*, Benedict had arranged to meet Spielberg at his suite at the Connaught Hotel.

He headed over to Mayfair on his motorbike, but when he got there, he couldn't find anywhere to park. He went round the block again and again, before finally spotting a space. By now, he was running way behind schedule and by the time he got to the hotel he was unbelievably late. "I went in with my shoulders up saying 'Sorry, so sorry,' and Steven was just so sweet," he remembers. A week and a half later, Benedict got another call from his agent: "'Ben, he wants you to do it.' I was so excited. It was the most grown-up moment of my life. I was told I couldn't tell anyone, so I was walking around with this huge grin on my face and couldn't speak with excitement."

The story of *War Horse* begins in England on the eve of the First World War. A struggling farming family purchases a fiery hunter colt at an auction; named Joey, the horse seems to be nothing but trouble for Ted and Rosie Narracott, though their son Albert is determined to tame and train the spirited animal. Albert and Joey become inseparable, but when war breaks out, the horse is sold and taken away to the Front. Thus Joey sets out on a remarkable journey, one on which he will experience great hardship and sorrow as well as friendship and joy. The horse becomes a remarkable symbol of hope, touching lives on both sides of the conflict with his innocence and unconditional devotion to human friends. He pulls battlefield ambulances, carries away German soldiers and inspires the devotion of a French girl. As his original owner, Albert, heads into the trenches on his own dangerous mission, Joey finds himself trapped in the barbed wire of No Man's Land between the British and German lines. But even when it seems his fate is sealed, the horse sets in motion a chain of remarkable events that eventually sees him reunited with Albert and returning to the family farm in England.

For many, *War Horse* tells an important story, one that still has great relevance a century after the events it describes. It first found fame as a well-loved family book, then as an innovative stage play, and now, with Spielberg in charge, was set to become a blockbuster movie. It all started when children's author Michael Morpurgo decided he wanted to write a tale set against the backdrop of the Great War. Morpurgo had been looking for a novel way to write about the conflict, but it wasn't until he met an aged veteran that he saw a way in. The veteran talked with passion, not about his fellow soldiers, but about the loyal and brave horses that he had served with. Like most people, Morpurgo had never even considered the role of wartime horses, but this old man changed that as he spoke of the bonds between soldiers and their mounts that kept so many going when they might otherwise have given up. "Here I was listening to this old man who had tears in his eyes talking about a relationship he had with a horse on the Western Front decades ago," Morpurgo recalls. "I learned that these horses were doing so much more than simply carrying soldiers or gun carriages. They deeply mattered to people."

Morpurgo set about researching the matter and discovered that a remarkable one million horses were sent into battle with the British during the First World War while only 62,000 returned. He learned how important horses were on all sides of the conflict, and read historical accounts of how horses suffered and committed acts of bravery, just like their human owners. Published in 1982 as a story for young adults, *War Horse* quickly became popular around the world. In 2007, when the novel was adapted into a stage play at London's National Theatre, audiences were quick to embrace its enduring themes of human-animal friendship, perseverance and the power of hope.

The play grabbed the imagination of producer Kathleen Kennedy: "I couldn't get the story and the emotions it evoked out of my head," she recalls. She instantly thought of Spielberg, knowing he had all the creative [ability] in a universal and contemporary way. "Steven wasn't interested in resources to find the way to bring this astonishing story to moviegoers making a war movie," explains Kennedy. "Rather, what he loved about *War Horse* was the relationship between the boy and this horse and their journey. Everybody can identify with Joey's primal emotions and, as a result, cannot help but care deeply for what happens to him, and by following Joey's experience, Steven could show the goodness to be found in people fighting on either side in the war."

From the outset, Kennedy anticipated that the power of Spielberg's approach would be his ability to home in on the ordinary relationships that allow people to rise above their circumstances. Morpurgo was thrilled at Spielberg's involvement and his sensitive direction: "There was an incredible meeting of minds with Steven. We're both storytellers who are fascinated by how stories can expand and grow. Steven told the story in his own way, with more depth and breadth."

The London-based executive producer Revel Guest – who had wanted to make a film of *War Horse* since seeing the play – also expressed her satisfaction: "There is no one I can think of that we would prefer to have direct this film than Steven Spielberg," she raved. "He is a lover of horses and also the best war director of our times, so the two combined is exactly right."

The filmmakers now set to adapting the novel. British screenwriter Lee Hall was brought in, and then, to add more layers, they brought in another Brit, Richard Curtis. The story, Curtis believes, has a strong connection to current world events. "With the financial recession, and the threat of terrorism, that question of how individuals survive in a big, dangerous world is something that we are all more aware of right now."

The screenwriters had a challenge on their hands. How could Joey remain at the very centre of the story despite having no voice; and how could the narrative stay with Joey's desire to get home without becoming mired in the chaos of the war? "The war had to be a presence which you always know is there, a threat, but not the central subject," says Curtis. "The challenge was achieving a balance, not diminishing the horror of the war but not eclipsing what is a very moving story about people bound together by a horse."

When the darkness of war arrives in Devon, Albert and Joey are forced apart, but Spielberg and Curtis found a narrative device to tie the two friends together even as they go their separate ways. This became the pennant Albert ties to Joey's reins the day he leaves for the Front. "I wanted to find a way to tie up all of the film's stories with one thing that becomes a kind of unifying force and that is the father's war pennant," says Spielberg. "Joey takes with him this memento of their relationship and it goes from story to story until the very end. It was very important to me that there be that kind of visual talisman. The campaign pennant connects Joey not only to all these other stories but it also connects the boy to his father and home."

Benedict was exactly what Spielberg was looking for to play the heroic cavalry officer, Major Jamie Stewart. Filming would begin well after *Frankenstein* had finished its run. And just as well. Benedict and several other members of the cast would have to take emergency riding lessons to prepare them for their roles. In some ways, the roles would be as physical as the ones Benedict had played alongside Jonny Lee Miller.

However, while learning to ride for the film's action scenes, Benedict's horse nearly brought a promising career to a sticky end. "I couldn't ride. I'd had a go at it when I was 12, but I wasn't very good at it. So I had to learn to do it properly. There are these amazing delicate instructions going on between man and animal, it's magic. To get a horse to hit a mark without a rider, to get it to stand up, to get it to rear, to get it to pick up a bucket and bring it over is amazing. It's hard work and very rewarding but can be dangerous. One day, my horse, called Faldo, reared and I thought it was game over. I was charging around on him, showjumping and picking up stuff and dropping it off. I think I just went for it too much, and accidentally gave him a confusing instruction, kicking him as well as reining him back. He thought I meant for him to stand up and the next thing I know he started going. I made the classic mistake of pulling on the reins to keep my seat and he started to go backwards, which is really dangerous because he was about to fall backwards on top of me. That was a near miss. The day before I had a horse that spooked on me and just bolted and it was really scary. My horse saw a movement and was galloping along and just ground to halt. There were hoof skid marks in the ground. It was very worrying. It turned out it was only a butterfly but it was pretty terrifying to be on a 17-and-a-half hand stallion doing an emergency stop."

But despite the training, there would still be some scenes in which the actors would be replaced by stunt doubles, which according to Benedict would be used for the most dangerous equestrian sequences. "They have to be there. You can't insure actors to do it. When I hear Daniel Craig, and everyone, talking about doing their own stunts, I think it's bullshit." Even though that is probably true, criticizing the likes of Craig seemed quite uncharacteristic of what Benedict would say in an interview.

According to most journalists who have met the actor, Benedict is ridiculously and unfailingly polite – he remembers names, recalls previous meetings, shows an interest, gives every question deep consideration and attends to the demands of hungry-for-information reporters. According to friend Matthew Goode, "he likes to follow a point through to the end. He's able to get from point A to point B and finish it with extreme clarity." It is also down to a feeling he has of being misrepresented by the press, and it's only by giving the exact line, his exact position, without distraction, that he can hope not to be misquoted. Much of his carefulness is said to have stemmed from when he told the *Radio Times* that he felt "castigated" for his privileged background, which then found its way into the tabloids. "All the posh-baiting that goes on is just so predictable, so domestic, so dumb."

According to his own definition of himself, "I'm an upper middle-class kid. I know that's counted as posh, but then I know people who I would call posh, and I don't talk like them." Although the comment may seem defensive to some, was it really? He has every reason on Earth to want to ensure that the public's perception of him is the right one. That's because, his cutting files are littered with occasionally tetchy exchanges with interviewers. Even a cover story in the *Hollywood Reporter*, which proclaimed him the key player of "The New A-List", was awkward when the writer started his article with, "I am 45 minutes into an interview with Benedict Cumberbatch, and frankly, it's not going well."

In many ways, it sounded as if Benedict was toughening up, and who can blame him. That same edge was on display when *Big Issue* writer Laura Kelly asked him how it felt to be the next big thing. "I've been the next big thing for 10 years," was how he replied, somewhat caustically. On another occasion, while filming *Sherlock*, he held up a piece of paper to the paparazzi hovering nearby that read, "Go photograph Egypt and show the world something more important!" As far as Benedict was concerned, "I was really shocked with what was going on, so I just thought if this culture is so fixated on me, I may as well use it to ask questions. I wasn't trying to trash popular culture. I don't belittle the appetites of people who just want to see shots of Sherlock," he sighed. "I guess that's my nearest flirtation with social media, and if I get misinterpreted in print, or if the perception of me is edited in print, then this is clear, I'm holding up the words."

But if he was indeed toughening up, then perhaps he had his reasons. Far away from the camera, the public spotlight and the big stages and film sets, maybe things in Benedict's private life weren't going as well as he had expected. Although he and Olivia Poulet had been together for a decade –notwithstanding a few separations – and had lived together in Hampstead in north London, perhaps now their life together was coming to an end.

If that was true, it couldn't have come at a worse time. Individually their careers couldn't have been better. Benedict was playing classic roles on both stage and screen, and Olivia was making tabloid headlines playing Camilla Parker Bowles opposite Laurence Fox as Prince Charles in ITV's royal romance *Whatever Love Means*. After that she had made a name for herself in cutting-edge TV shows such as *Outnumbered* and *Love Soup* as well as the political drama, *The Thick of It* and its big screen adaptation *In the Loop*. But successful careers don't always make for a happy relationship, especially in showbusiness.

With time at a premium for both, the idea of getting married and starting a family seemed to become more and more of a remote possibility. Certainly, Benedict had often spoken out publicly about his desire to become a parent and was now becoming more and more broody. "I've always wanted kids. I'm very broody," he told *The Times* reporter Patricia Nicol as far back as 2005. His feelings didn't diminish. In 2011, when he was asked – at the age of 32 – to reveal his greatest disappointment, he replied, without any hesitation, that it was not being a dad by the age of 32. It probably didn't help that most of his friends now had two point three children, which Benedict is said to enjoy entertaining and spending time with during his off-time in his not-so-public role of honorary uncle.

But after 10 years with Olivia, and no sign of children on the horizon or a dream wedding about to happen, perhaps it was no surprise when he and Olivia decided to go their separate ways. The split, however, was not for public consumption. The couple wanted to avoid any fuss or tabloid headlines, and didn't give any interviews or pose for any photos before, during or after the break-up. When the press did get curious about what had gone wrong, Benedict's publicist released a very brief statement confirming that, yes, the couple had split amicably and that no further comment would be made. But that, of course, didn't stop the press intrusion.

Not that Benedict was alone for long. Close friends from the set of *Downton Abbey* Dan Stevens and Michelle Dockery were among the many who flocked around to help the actor cope. He tried to spend more time in the kitchen, and was often seen buying provisions at Giacobazzi's, an Italian delicatessen near his home in Hampstead. On his days off, he followed *Sherlock* co-star Martin Freeman's example and started wandering around charity shops looking for anything from shoes to suits. Then he hit the big department stores with credit card in hand. "I've been quite a late developer on the clothes front but I've suddenly realized it's one of life's joys." He was often spotted browsing at vintage store Beyond Retro. He headed to the edgy east and took in some sample sales at The Old Truman Brewery on Brick Lane where he was seen buying T-shirts, some with original prints and other arty one-offs. Back at home, he and friends enjoyed nights in watching box sets of classic shows like *The Wire*, *The Office*, *The West Wing*, *Mad Men* and *The Sopranos*.

Even if he declared being single was fun, he was not entirely convinced. Like so many other singles, he soon came to acknowledge, in his private moments, that it wasn't always as great as it was made out to be. "When I was last single, I wasn't the same person." He was reminded of his early days at Manchester University, when he says he had a blast with girls, drinking and clubbing.

All the same, Benedict still missed the proximity of a partnership with someone he knew and loved. Plus, playing the dating game would not be easy. "It's hard because people think they know more about you than they actually do. And you can't control that. You can't control perceptions of you." Matthew Goode agrees. "He's not that old, but he's coming to the end of his 30s, so he's looking for a long-term partner, but if he has to have a few conquests to get to the right one, I'm sure the cream of the crop will be coming towards him. He's going to enjoy himself."

But unlike so many other newly single individuals, he had plenty of other distractions lined up in 2010 and 2011. Almost without noticing, he was fast turning into one of the busiest actors in Britain. The radio gigs that had seen him through quite a few quiet patches in the past were coming in thick and fast. He was also in demand for voice-overs for commercials. His so-called "brushed-suede vowels" won him a lot of one-off gigs that could be wrapped up in less than a day and give him financial freedom for months, if not years. He was also back on the big screen, albeit for less than two minutes of screen time, playing an American police officer in *The Whistleblower* opposite Rachel Weisz. Then, just when he needed it most, he secured his biggest part yet. He was going to be part of one of the biggest film trilogies of the moment. He was going to Middle Earth.

Like any other boy, Benedict loved having bedtime stories read to him as a youngster. He remembers his actor-father bringing stories to life with a never-ending variety of voices and accents and among the books he enjoyed having read to him was *The Hobbit* by J R R Tolkien, a tale Benedict admits was a favourite. You can imagine how thrilled he must have been at the prospect of stepping into a movie version of the tale. Even better, was the news that the film was being made by Peter Jackson, one of the world's most important filmmakers. The director's *The Lord of the Rings* trilogy is still ranked as the most successful trilogy of movies ever made, and collectively won an unprecedented 17 of its 30 Academy Award nominations, including Best Picture for the final instalment.

If that wasn't enough, Benedict must have been thrilled when he heard that Ian McKellan, who was returning to resume the role he played in *The Lord of the Rings* and had worked with Benedict's father in 1966 and his mother in 2005, had been blown away by the actor's screen test. "I was shown a snippet of his screen-test, played in close-up into the camera. It was electrifying, vocally and facially," he said, though at the time he had no idea which character Benedict would be playing. Neither did Jackson, but agreeing with McKellan's comments, he signed Benedict up to play both the Necromancer and the dragon Smaug, alongside his *Sherlock* co-star Martin Freeman, who got top billing as Bilbo Baggins (which in turn, turned Freeman into a fully-fledged movie star).

First published in September 1937, *The Hobbit* has sold more than 100 million copies and has been translated into around 50 languages. Written by the revered author and poet J R R Tolkien – as a bedtime story for his children – the text reveals the author's love of fairytales, his experiences of war, and his sense of affinity with those who fight against seemingly insurmountable odds.

The adventure follows the epic journey of Bilbo Baggins on his quest to take back the lost Dwarf Kingdom of Erebor from the fearsome dragon Smaug. After being approached by the wizard Gandalf the Grey, Bilbo joins a company of 13 dwarves led by the legendary warrior Thorin Oakenshield. Together they journey into the Wild, passing through treacherous lands and encountering Goblins, Orcs and deadly Wargs, as well as a sinister figure known only as the Necromancer.

Despite countless adaptations in a variety of media, *The Hobbit* had never been fully realized as a movie until Peter Jackson decided to take it on. He was probably the only filmmaker with the right measure of skill, passion and dedication to now do the story justice and bring it to life on the big screen.

The adventure of filming down under, however, was far from easy. Known as the king of back-to-back filming, Jackson would produce the film and its sequel in one long shoot and then edit it into two distinct halves. But the plan for *The Hobbit* became more complex when the two films turned into three, and filming effectively went back to back to back – in much the same way as had happened with the second and third instalments of Jerry Bruckheimer's *Pirates of the Caribbean* movies (starring Johnny Depp, and Benedict's *Atonement* co-star, Keira Knightley).

Part of the allure for Benedict was that Jackson's films always did great business at the box office. They push their stars into a new level of fame and, at the same time, open plenty more doors for them in the future. Then, of course, there was the part itself. Benedict's key role of Smaug was of course that of a dragon, allowing him to stretch himself professionally. In the past, his research for a new part involved meeting people, talking to experts and reading a lot of intense biographies. For Smaug, it involved going to London Zoo to watch the Komodo dragons. "I've been going there to see how the skeleton moves differently, what the head movements are like," he said, smiling at the sheer fun of it all. He concluded that the vital task was to get the posture right. "He crouches forward, swivelling his eyes snakily, to demonstrate," one reporter said after meeting him just before he left London.

Certainly, the big budget *Hobbit* films were peopled by typically big-name stars. Benedict would ultimately share the bill with the likes of Cate Blanchett and Christopher Lee. But he didn't get to meet them on set. Most of the time, he acted almost alone, against a green screen with just Jackson calling the shots and shouting out his instructions. The set itself was vast, effectively a giant empty warehouse. Benedict had to suit up in specialist clothing that would record his moves. Four static cameras and a wall of sensors watched him, and the information from that would be fed into computers to generate the image we would ultimately see on screen. Even though Smaug was very far from being human, he would still, very clearly, be Benedict Cumberbatch.

"I was very lucky to work with Pete," he raved. "As far as the experience, what an extraordinary one it was, because at the time I was in my work, I was in isolation with him and this incredible tag team. And at the very cool place with that technology doing mocap [motion capture] for two characters, and it was an awful lot of fun. It's a sort of wonderful ongoing process. I spent a lot of time recording the voice as well as doing movements. So, it was sort of freeing, it was fun. It was like playing a game. It's going to be an amazing film, it's going to be a real treat. I watched *The Lord of the Rings* again before I started working, and the way those films grow in depth of craft on every level are extraordinary." Filming *The Hobbit* certainly brought challenges of a different kind. Benedict plays two roles, the Necromancer and Smaug (a fantastical villain he describes as "a 400-year-old fire-breathing worm who lives in the middle of a mountain on top of a pile of gold, who is three or four times bigger than the Empire State Building and can fly"), both of which he created without having other actors to play off. He described the experience of working on his scenes with the director, Peter Jackson, wearing a motion-capture suit. "It's sort of a grey all-in-one jumpsuit, with a skullcap, a Madonna headset and Aboriginal-like face paint. You feel like a tit in all that gear but Peter is so lovely you soon forget."

Most of the work Benedict did for Peter Jackson in 2011 would remain unseen for some time. Martin Freeman would dominate the first film of the trilogy and Benedict's Smaug wouldn't get much screen time until the release of *The Desolation of Smaug* in late 2013. By then, both men would be in demand like never before, but even in 2011, they had enough clout to see the New Zealand set effectively put on hold while they flew back to the UK to complete their commitments on series two of *Sherlock*. Luckily Jackson was happy to release them. "Peter completely understands *Sherlock* and loves it," Benedict said gratefully.

Benedict was pretty star-struck himself when he discovered another *Sherlock* fan in the shape of David Bowie. "He's obsessed with it,' said Benedict. "That is so fucking cool!" Equally cool for the actor was the chance to go skydiving on a break from filming *The Hobbit*. It was, he assured people, "an incredibly horny experience."

Back in Britain, Benedict's mad merry-go-round was about to speed up even more. Most actors might take a rest with three more 90-minute episodes of *Sherlock* in the bag, a major film trilogy being put together and a Spielberg film going through its final edits. But no, Benedict wanted more. Matthew Goode remembers when he turned up at his house after finishing something at the National Theatre, and yet another film. "My wife said, 'How are you Ben?' And he said, 'Yeh, um, I'm all right, I mean I'm unemployed at the moment.' He had been unemployed for two days!" It seems if he wasn't working, he was quite lost. Not that he had to worry with another movie project lined up. And this time, it was for the kind of role Benedict had always longed to play. But it very nearly went horribly wrong.

The near-disaster came when Benedict was called to the offices of Working Title, the company behind the all-star remake of *Tinker Tailor Soldier Spy*. Tomas Alfredson, the Swedish director best known at the time for his vampire tale, *Let the Right One In*, greeted Benedict warmly and asked him what he thought of the script. The only problem was that Benedict hadn't seen it, let alone read it. There had apparently been a mix-up with its delivery. Alfredson just stared at Benedict, open-mouthed, as if he was in shock. Benedict was sure he would be sent packing and be told never to turn up for a casting unprepared again. Having been late for his vital meeting with Spielberg, he didn't feel he could recover from a second disaster.

The Swedish director, however, was relaxed enough to cope with the situation. He asked Benedict to do a read through there and then, and according to insiders, the actor did it flawlessly. The end result, of course, was that he won the pivotal and multi-faceted role of Peter Guillam, the tortured gay spy who is right in the midst of the search for the mole at M16. It was a powerful, infinitely controlled performance, all the stronger for the fact that every piece of emotion had to be shown, but held firmly in check. Benedict of course, loved it. "I've always wanted to play a spy, because it is the ultimate acting exercise. You are never what you seem."

His enthusiasm was understandable. As Guillam, Benedict has to supervise M16's scalp hunters, the spies who do the agency's dirty work. He is loyal to the Circus, Britain's elite espionage force but also to George Smiley, played by Gary Oldman, one of the agency's leaders and a parental figure to Guillam. One of the many secrets Guillam keeps is his sexual orientation – he has an established relationship with an older man and the two share a home. Throughout the film, Guillam struggles with loyalty and betrayal, at work and at home, and ultimately must decide to whom he will give his loyalty and how he will deal with the consequences of betrayal.

Within the Circus, Peter Guillam has been brought up in the shadow of his bosses, played by Toby Jones, Colin Firth, David Dencik and Ciarán Hinds, who work for the all-powerful leader, Control (John Hurt). After Control is forced out in a power struggle, his right-hand man Smiley is also sent into retirement. When a mole within the Circus needs to be found, Smiley is brought out of retirement to determine which of his former colleagues is a Soviet double agent. Because Smiley can trust Guillam, he secretly enlists the younger man's help in a dangerous undercover assignment. Guillam is asked to go against all he holds dear in order to spy on "his own" and help destroy the mole.

The idea that someone subversive can hide in plain sight and fool even his closest companions takes on two meanings in Guillam's story. He believes in the organization for which he works and is sickened by the idea that someone who has mentored him may be a traitor. Even worse is the thought that he himself might be perceived as a traitor to the organization, simply because he is gay.

Even though *Tinker Tailor Soldier Spy* indicated a change in Benedict's movie profile and status, John Le Carré was not that enthusiastic about a remake. Well, not initially, anyway. In fact, he approached the prospect of a feature film of his bestselling spy novel with the same misgivings that would have afflicted anyone else who had loved the 1979 TV series. As far as he was concerned, the role of George Smiley belonged to Alec Guinness and Alec was George.

"How could another actor equal let alone surpass him?" says the author. "And how could any movie director, even one as distinguished as Tomas Alfredson, tell the same intricate story in a couple of hours? The television series had needed seven episodes. And slice it how you will, television drama is still radio with pictures, whereas feature film these days barely talks at all. My anxieties were misplaced. Alfredson has delivered a film that for me works superbly, and takes me back into byways of the novel and its characters that the series of 32 years ago didn't enter. Gary Oldman's Smiley pays full honour to the genius of Guinness. He evokes the same solitude, inwardness, pain and intelligence that his predecessor brought to the part – even the same elegance. But Oldman's Smiley, from the moment he appears, is a man waiting patiently to explode. The danger, the pressed-down fury and the humanity that almost doesn't manage to keep its head above the parapet of despair, are Oldman's own. If I were to meet the Smiley of Alec Guinness on a dark night, my instinct would be to go to his protection. If I met Oldman's, I think I just might make a run for it. The film, through my very personal prism, is a triumph. And if people write to me and say 'How could you let this happen to poor Alec Guinness,' I shall reply that 'if poor Alec had witnessed Oldman's performance, he would have been the first to give it a standing ovation.' It's not the film of the book. It's the film of the film, and to my eye a work of art in its own right. I'm very proud to have provided Alfredson with the material, but what he made of it is wonderfully his own."

Alfredson didn't have any such concerns. "When I first met John, he was very clear about his wishes regarding the film version of his novel. Please don't shoot the book or remake the TV mini-series. They already exist. I'm not going to interfere, but you can call me any time if there is anything you wonder about. I think we have obeyed him to the letter. Of course, you cannot encompass every detail in a book of 349 pages at the movies. But you can take themes and strands and moments, and try to describe what you see. With *Tinker Tailor Soldier Spy*, I think we've made a film about loyalty and ideals, values that are extremely relevant, perhaps mostly because they are so rare these days."

Benedict prepared for his role in his customary manner. Not only did he take on his usual amount of reading, and he also boarded a plane for Morocco. His character, Peter Guillam, had been a North Africa expert, so it was only fitting that he discovered for himself what that may have been like. "It was the first time I had ever gone on holiday on my own," he says, and he made the most of it. At night, he walked the streets of the North African town he was staying in, a lone Englishman trying to feel how Guillam might have felt a generation or two before. When he wasn't doing that, he was kite-surfing – but that, he openly admits was more about getting an adrenaline high rather than putting in the perfect performance as a Cold War spy.

Once filming had been completed and the cinema-going public waited for the releases of both *War Horse* and *Tinker Tailor Soldier Spy*, the unexpected happened. A New York producer called Benedict. He wanted him to go to Broadway to reprise his role in *After the Dance*. Even though Benedict had always dreamed of appearing on Broadway, he shocked everyone by turning the opportunity down, simply because film was where he saw his immediate future. "I've never really made a head-over-heart decision like that before," he explained. "It does seem as though I have a bit of momentum at the moment, and while I love theatre, it is always a huge commitment and I'd like to keep myself available for more film work."

Not only that, but far from the public eye, Benedict had started dating again. Although he and Olivia remained good friends, and had nothing but nice things to say about each other – and in Benedict's mind, they will always be on good terms with each other – it was time to move on to pastures new. The press had finally stopped focusing on the slight oddness of his features, and instead, gave him the full sex-symbol status. "It puts a bit of a spring in your step," he admitted. Even if he thought he was punching above his weight when it came to looks and girls, fans disagreed. Certainly, his new confidence showed when he met Anna Jones, a tall, dark-haired fashion designer from London. Although the relationship was kept very lowkey, that didn't stop the couple being spotted out at restaurants and social events that autumn.

Having successfully made his way through the minefield of dating in his mid-30s, Benedict felt able to walk a little taller and speak a little louder with Anna on his arm. But was there another reason for shunning Broadway in favour of Hollywood? If so, it was rooted in the past. The latent competitiveness of an English public school education had come back into play. The rugby-mad sportsman in Benedict wanted to be a winner. He was close to the top of the TV tree with *Sherlock*. But while he had been filming in south Wales, he had seen many of his contemporaries make their names in Hollywood. Fellow thirtysomethings such as James McAvoy, Michael Fassbender and Ben Whishaw were all "working their way to the big table, and I wouldn't mind a little taste of that."

The critics were on his side. Many claimed that if his highly nuanced performance in *Tinker Tailor* is a taste of what's to come, then he would surely be dining at the top table for quite a while. Sure, he too was on the big screen in a British spy thriller, and he was going to be in Steven Spielberg and Peter Jackson's latest movies. However, the former had been a very British affair and the latter had its roots down under. The beating heart of entertainment was still on the west coast of America and, if nothing else, Benedict wanted to discover if he had what it takes to be a star out there too.

In early 2012, the actor was about to find out. The second series of *Sherlock* was about to be screened and, as expected, anticipation levels were running high. Rumours about the plot of the opening episode had already reached fever pitch and the show's ratings were set to go through the roof. Benedict was about to become a bona fide star in Hollywood.

Chapter 9
In and Out of Darkness

More than eight million people tuned in to watch the primetime *Sherlock* show on New Year's Day 2012. It didn't just trend on Twitter, talk of the show dominated many other social networking sites for days. It became one of the BBC's biggest-ever programmes on catch-up TV as people watched it later in the week, or took a second glance. It could, of course, have been a massive anti-climax. It might have gone off on an impossible tangent and disappointed audiences. But it didn't.

The first episode of the second Sherlock series, "A Scandal in Belgravia", would thrill the tabloids for weeks. We watched Sherlock meet the fabulous Irene Adler (played by Lara Pulver), we saw Benedict's total command of his character, and we had nudity, political intrigue, gratuitous royalty and endless in-jokes about the nature of Sherlock's relationship with Dr Watson. We loved it.

Much of the fuss in the "A Scandal in Belgravia" episode seem to stem from the moment viewers are properly introduced to Irene Adler. In the original story, "A Scandal in Bohemia", Adler blackmails foreign royalty and battles Holmes, whose client seeks the return of an incriminating photograph. In the end she escapes into marriage and Holmes has possession of the photograph. In the twenty-first-century version, Adler is a professional dominatrix who collects scandalous photographs of some of her more famous clients. Soon Sherlock and Watson find themselves whisked to Buckingham Palace where Mycroft Holmes informs them they need to recover compromising photographs of someone whom Holmes deduces is a member of the Royal Family. Intriguingly Adler is not asking for money at first, deepening the mystery. Eventually Sherlock and Watson confront Adler. She already knows they're coming, however, and greets Sherlock while totally in the nude.

Shooting that scene, says Lara Pulver, was a logistical nightmare. "We were lucky with our DP [Director of Photography] and our first-camera operator. We spent eight hours doing the scene. It was a situation where I could have worn a thong and nipple covers, but we probably would have been there for three days, trying to shoot around that stuff. The director said, 'Lara, if you trust me, I'll ask you to take that stuff off and know that we can't use anything of that nature, anyway. We'll get a lot more done in a lot less time, and we'll all be more comfortable.' And he was totally right, so I'm glad I trusted him on that judgement. It's brilliant, how literally a head turn covers a nipple. It's pretty well placed. I was thrilled with the outcome. I was happy."

But despite drawing in almost nine million viewers on the night, the episode also attracted 100 complaints. "It was literally one newspaper in the UK, and a few viewers," remembers Pulver. "With nine and a half million viewers, a few people were upset. I think there's something to embrace about flesh. It's human. We came into this world naked. It's literally a couple of minutes in a 90-minute episode, and it's not about, 'Oh, there's a naked scene in *Sherlock*.' It's totally a device. If it wasn't, I wouldn't have done it."

"To be honest," she continues, "I think I was extremely nervous and adrenaline was running. It was the first time I've ever had to be completely naked, in anything. And then, after the first couple of takes, I found the power in being a woman without hiding behind a dress or Spanx, or trying to give off any illusion of being thinner or fatter or more beautiful, because I was actually completely vulnerable and stripped of any of that. And then, I found a different power that came from a very honest place, and we just played from there. By the end of it, I wouldn't move from a certain aspect of dialogue until Martin Freeman had looked me up and down, or looked at my breasts. It was a play fest."

Pulver had landed the role while she was doing an episode of *Spooks*. Well, sort of. "I had just wrapped on it and they gave me the script for *Sherlock* to have a little read on the plane. I was reading it on the plane, and I literally wanted to turn the plane back around. On the page, it was such a good script. So, I arrived back in LA and put myself down on tape, reading the scenes, sent them over and they responded. A few days later, I flew back to London to meet the producer and read with Benedict. I got the job the next day, and started rehearsals a few days later. I had read some Sir Arthur Conan Doyle when I was in high school. And then, the next time it crossed my path was when I was watching Season 1 here, on PBS. I just loved this modern interpretation that Steven Moffat and Mark Gatiss had put together because it just doesn't underestimate its audience, which I love. It's intelligent and witty and mischievous, and I love what Benedict and Martin have brought to the show, as their Sherlock and Watson. I think it's integral, and I think they'll go down as a very highly rated television duo."

"But they're naughty little boys", she continues. "They're very funny, and they are very different. Martin is very naughty. Just the nature of the lines that Benedict has to deliver, it's a big task for him. It's not easy, having to scroll off all of that stuff, at such a pace. Playing clever isn't always that easy. But, it was thrilling to work with them both. They're both very playful and responsive. Martin, especially, will throw you completely different interpretations of scenes, all the time. It brings so many different colours to the scene, which makes it really interesting to go to work. If I had any concerns at all about it, I was slightly anxious about being any sort of love interest, when people were already so attached to the fact that Benedict's Sherlock was asexual or gay, or whatever they wanted to project onto his performance. I was like, Oh, my god, all the female fans are probably going to hate me! But, what was lovely was that, the day I turned up to do the table read, they had just come off the back of a huge, roaring success of a first season with Emmy nominations and BAFTA awards, and there was such a lovely, quiet confidence in that room. Not only were these people working at the top of their game, but they were also being recognized for it and celebrating what they collaboratively had put together. So, I walked in and it was just such a comfortable place to go to work, where egos were left at the door. It was just all about the work, from every angle."

The one thing that did surprise Adler, however was the set. "When I walked into 221B, I thought, 'This is really small!' I know it's a set, but it felt much bigger when I had watched it, just from the camera angles. I thought it was quite vast, but when I walked in, I was like, 'Oh, this is a pokey little flat!' I remember one day, when we were shooting in London on location and I had to pull back the curtain on the window, and all I saw on the opposite side of the street was about 150 fans, out of shot. I thought, 'Wow, that's their dedication to three episodes of this show!' That shows what an impact this show is having."

Of course, she was right. The show was having a huge impact. Even if the second series was as short and sweet as the first, it was still a massive hit. The second episode, "The Hounds of Baskerville", is probably the most famous of all the Sherlock Holmes mysteries, and it was a clever idea by Moffat and Gattis to give the original title just the smallest of tweaks and then have their wicked way with the rest of the tale. Baskerville this time was not a crumbly house but a dodgy animal experimentation centre kept out of the way of prying eyes on the moors. "Hound" was no beast but the acronym for an even dodgier drugs programme that made people hallucinate their worst nightmares to the degree that they thought they were actually taking place, and yes, there was a big bad dog too. The original had a villain called Stapleton; there was a Stapleton here as well but, although a bit snarly, she wasn't the one doing the really devilish deeds.

Then there was just one more 90-minute episode to enjoy. And it was a classic. With Andrew Scott playing the perfect baddie, Jim Moriarty, the writers gave viewers an excellent cliffhanger of an ending to series two in "The Reichenbach Fall" with Sherlock seemingly leaping to his death from a London rooftop and then appearing at his own graveside. After that episode aired, it seemed as if everyone in the world was trying to figure out how exactly television's most popular sleuth survived, and why he kept the truth about his fate from his grieving friend John Watson. For almost two years, Sherlock's rooftop leap prompted much freeze-framing, head scratching and theorizing as viewers dreamt up various explanations for how the Baker Street genius managed to cheat death. The most popular three theories were that it hadn't been Sherlock at all; that the detective had broken his fall; and that Watson had been hallucinating.

Benedict was as curious as the nation was to figure it out. "I had my own idea and it wasn't far off," he told reporters a few weeks before the first episode of series three, "The Empty Hearse" was to be shown. "It was as surprising and delightful when I read about it in the script as I hope the audience will find it. I think I sort of got into the same obsession that the nation did, before we did it. But without meaning to patronize at all, my personal preference is being surprised in the moment of watching something rather than knowing ahead of time, but I also understand why everyone's desperate to know because it's frustrating."

The reviews for series two were as strong as ever throughout the run of three episodes over three weekends. It was clear Benedict's life was changing for the better. One reporter met him in a north London pub just before the first episode was broadcast when Benedict was still almost anonymous, and was drinking nothing stronger than coffee. But he was just as wired as ever. "He chatters freely with rapier speed – one thing he shares with his on-screen alter-ego. Post *Sherlock*, he has metamorphosed into something bigger and odder. A pin-up. Odder, that is, because Benedict, with his long face, blanched skin and very pale blue eyes, is not a conventional heartthrob. You can see why he was as much at ease playing the monster and his creator in the National's recent adaptation of *Frankenstein*. And yet, the swooning web interest in him is legion, from the Twitter collective devoted to his daily appreciation, to endless blogs, forums and fan sites."

The online madness presented a new challenge for Benedict. Do you read the gossip and risk being burned? Or do you bury your head in the sand and think ignorance is bliss? Lots of actors say you should avoid every review – and possibly every interview. They say that the benefit from 20 positive reviews can be destroyed by a single bad word in the twenty-first one. But as the cyber-chatter got even louder Benedict did decide to take a look. He read some of the latest very adult fan fiction. He blushed. "Weird," was all he could say before logging off. But with a smile.

Back in the real world, his madly crazy life continued. His parents had taught him that an actor's life can have plenty of empty patches. There can be an awful lot of time resting and waiting tables to make ends meet. And then there can be high-voltage months when everything seems to happen at once. January 2012 became one of those months that would turn out to be just like every month of that year. It seemed that 2012 belonged to Benedict Cumberbatch.

It all kicked off that January. The second series of *Sherlock* topped the ratings far beyond expectations, and the star-studded premiere at the Odeon Leicester Square of *War Horse* was attended by Prince William and the Duchess of Cambridge. The film had already grossed an unexpected $80 million at the US box office and was well on its way to taking twice that amount at box offices around the world. As if that wasn't enough, there was something even bigger waiting in the wings.

Just before Christmas, Benedict had received a call telling him that J J Abrams was interested in him playing the villain in the new *Star Trek* movie, *Star Trek Into Darkness*. Benedict wasn't the only actor that Abrams had considered for the role, but when Benedict's interpretation of the character took off in a completely unpredictable direction, Abrams came to the conclusion that the actor would be a perfect fit – even if the choice did defy expectations. Abrams was sold on what he had seen of Benedict's combination of skill and magnetism, both on the big screen and from his work in *Sherlock* – which by this time was already beginning to gather momentum in the US. The first season was pulling in an average

4.6 million viewers per episode. It all helped to show Abrams exactly what he would be getting for his money.

"In the first film [*Star Trek*], we had extraordinary actors who took these iconic roles and made them their own, with a spirit that completely validated what they were doing," Abrams explained. "And that's what Benedict did with his character for the second film. He came to the table with a whole new attitude, personality, background and strength. But he's such a compelling and powerful actor that it works. He has a wry sophistication to his approach that is so right. To me, it nullified any concerns of how he might look. We were not in any way undoing what's come before, but he is our version of this character. It was the right way to go because he was so damn good."

The only problem was Abrams needed to get Benedict on tape as soon as possible. "I got a call before Christmas Eve," remembers Benedict, "saying that they're very interested in you playing the not-so-good guy in the next *Star Trek* film, and can you get yourself on tape. I rang some friends of mine – and when I say friends, I mean the top-casting directors in England who were all on holiday because we observe this little Judeo-Christian cult holiday called Christmas. And the demands were coming in so fast, I was like, this is terrifying. And by the 27th, people were knocking on the door, literally, and saying I've got to put myself on tape. I was down in Gloucestershire with some friends, who turned out to be useless. I won't mention their names, they're quite well known friends, a director and a very brilliant actress. Bless them, they were busy with his kid. I then went down to London and begged my best friend there, Adam Ackland. He's always been there to put out the fire. And he said, 'Let's do it.'

"My Flip wasn't working, and I couldn't get any kind of recording device, so I said, I'm going to do it on my iPhone. It's high quality, it's HD. It will be fine. And so I ended up squatting in their kitchen, at about 11 o'clock at night. I was pretty strung out, so that went into the performance. And his wife, Alice, bless her, with two children asleep, was balancing two chairs to get the right angle on me and desk lamps bouncing light off bits of paper, just trying desperately to make it look half-decent, because it's going to go into J J Abrams's iPad. So we did it, and then it took a day and a half to compress it. I sent it to him, and then I got told, 'J J's on holiday.' I was furious. And then I heard on the day after New Year's Day. He sent me an e-mail, saying, 'You want to come and play?' I said, 'What does this mean? Are you in town, you want to go for a drink? I'm English, you've got to be really straight with me on this. Have I got the part?'"

Yes, he had. Both Abrams and Benedict were thrilled beyond words. Bryan Burk, Abrams's producing partner on *Star Trek* as well as on the TV show *Lost*, says the makeshift iPhone showreel hadn't harmed Benedict's chances one little bit. It was, he said, all about the scale of the screen. "Benedict has an incredible presence and brooding intensity. To say he's a welcome addition to the *Star Trek* cast is an understatement. He's an actor that truly captivates his audience." Abrams agreed. Benedict's iPhone tape was, he said, "one of the most compelling audition readings I'd ever seen."

Benedict's success was a timely reminder of the occasion he had been asked about his long-term ambitions, and his reply was simple. He wanted to play someone as far away from himself as possible, anyone from a mutated baddie in a comic-book action thriller to a detective, and if that was still true, then his ambition had just been fulfilled. Playing a still-to-be described baddie in the biggest sci-fi franchise of them all was perfect, and was about as far removed from the real Benedict as you could get. Not that he was ever a self-confessed Trekkie. In fact, he almost didn't go to see the first film.

"I wasn't that interested in seeing a *Star Trek* movie, I'll be honest. It's not out of any loathing of the genre or sci-fi or anything. I love it, but I just wasn't that interested. And people said, 'No, you should just go and see it. It's a great film.' And lo and behold, then all the Trekkie in me was reborn as well, and I was just over-the-moon excited about them all meeting for the first time. I thought it was such an imaginative prequel, but without a doubt, this one is truly epic. It's a big film. The scale of it is so much bigger than the first." Benedict was fully aware of the significance of the film and what it meant for lifelong *Star Trek* fans. "You can't try and fulfil everyone's expectations. As an actor, my role in this is to fulfil my director's promise in me and yeah, if I fulfil his trust in me, that's it. That's a job done. And then, I have full respect for the fans' response. I know that they own this. A lot of people have grown up with this all of their lives... And that is important to me, but if you go about trying to please everybody, it's a short way to madness."

Not that he had to worry – with J J Abrams at the helm, and Chris Pine and Zachary Quinto back in their roles as James T Kirk and Spock, how could the project fail? The story would pick up from where the first film left off, with the crew of the *Enterprise* being summoned home to Earth in the wake of a dreadful act of terror from within its own ranks. Breaking all the rules, Captain Kirk leads his crew on a manhunt to bring those responsible to justice. As the heroes find themselves sucked into an epic chess game of life and death, friendships will be torn apart, loyalties will be challenged and great sacrifices must be made.

Even in pre-production, the film sounded promising, and even more so with the news that it would be shot using extremely high-resolution IMAX cameras and presented in an expansively detailed 3D conversion that pushes the technology to give audiences a glimpse into the *Star Trek* universe as never seen before. There would be some $185 million spent to beat the near $400 million success of the 2009 blockbuster. So, while it was shrouded in typical Hollywood secrecy, everyone knew that *Into Darkness* would be one of the biggest films of 2013.

The only downside for Benedict was the news that shooting was to start immediately, which in Hollywood terms meant not today or tomorrow, but yesterday. It was a downside, because Benedict barely had time pack his bags and close down his life before heading off to Los Angeles. *Sherlock* was still showing on BBC when he slipped through Heathrow and boarded his plane to LAX airport in Los Angeles. When he got there, things weren't any easier. "I literally got off the plane and went straight to the studio. They were due to start shooting the film in five days. I walked into a room full of designers, artistic directors, editors, directors of photography and about five producers. I was terrified. I was jetlagged and must have looked as white as a sheet with dark rings round my eyes."

But his eyes lit up as soon as he looked around him. Right from the start he loved being on the Paramount Studios lot in Hollywood, still famous as the studio where Elvis Presley – a favourite of Benedict's – made some of his biggest pictures. "It's amazing," raved Benedict. "First an Egyptian walks by, then Lady Gaga, then somebody going to a game show." In the midst of it all was the cinematic juggernaught that was *Star Trek*. For the time he remained in LA, Benedict had to conform entirely to the film's unique vision. He moved into a house in the picturesque suburb of Venice, and got ready to go to work with his allocated personal trainer, nutritionist and fight choreographer. He ate 4,000 calories a day, spent two hours in the gym each day, did endless stunt rehearsals and went from a 38-inch to a 42-inch chest size. "I was playing with all those toys with J J Abrams at the helm, being dragged across the floor at nearly 50km an hour and beefing up. I went up four suit sizes in the space of a month. And I loved it." Even so, he was not someone who is naturally confident, by his own admittance. There are still moments, he says, when his confidence falters. The first day he stepped on set of the new *Star Trek* film, joining an illustrious line of British stars who have played the villain in a Hollywood blockbuster, he had a momentary feeling of being out of his depth. "I didn't know what I was going to do and I had very little time to establish the character in that franchise."

All the same, and as expected, Benedict says he had a ball on set. "It was wonderful to work with people my own age, all sharing an experience. I was the Brit abroad but everyone was incredibly supportive and welcoming." Working with J J Abrams added to the experience. As far as Benedict was concerned, Abrams was the true star of the film. "It's a very exciting set to be on. He's very imaginative, he's involved in all the details, the acting and all the wonderful ideas he has for capturing stories in a fresh and imaginative way. Just the range of stuff I get to do in one day, it's great." Not only that, he continues, "but what he's asking me is just wonderful. I can't say much nicer than that. I'm basically raving about it, and I don't have a gun pointed to my head."

"Certainly," continues Benedict, "he's a genuinely good human being, as well as being absurdly talented and popular. He's just fantastically talented, just in pay-offs and thrills and chills along the way. You kind of feel like you're in a travelling circus. There's a complete bleed between cast and crew and he brings incredible people on to inspire you – magicians, surgeons, veterans from the last two wars… just really extraordinary human beings. You learn a lot watching him work, because it's as much about how he does it as what he does – and what he does, I think, is supreme. But to spend time in his company, that's almost the biggest thrill of the job really. You come to crave the next scene, the next opportunity for you working together. He's a genius. He still has the fervour of a ten-year-old child when it comes to the enjoyment of what we do. It is, as a profession, a ridiculous privilege. But also he makes films that he wants to see, he's true to his tastes and he bears his responsibilities respectfully but lightly. You can get confidence from him and not worry about what he is worrying about. You can just go to him with your worries – you really need that as an actor. You need to be able to quell your anxieties about what you're doing, and the first point of call is the compactness of thought and temperament that your director provides you with. He's just off-the-charts brilliant at that. He does things with massive wedges of humour and the biggest thing at the heart of it all is that he's incredibly generous with his time and his care."

The plot of *Into Darkness* was being kept well under wraps when filming got underway. Everyone had to sign detailed non-disclosure agreements, and everything possible was done to stop leaks reaching the mass media. For example, Benedict assured *Access Hollywood*'s Scott Mantz that he wasn't playing the legendary villain Khan. "A few have asked me that which is strange," Benedict told Scott. He was joking about it being strange as it was wildly speculated he would play the youthful version of the character originated by Ricardo Montalban in a 1967 episode of the *Star Trek* television series *Space Seed*, and later, in the 1980s film *The Wrath of Khan*. "I play John Harrison who's a terrorist and an extraordinary character in his own right. He's somebody who is not your two-dimensional cookie-cutter villain. He's got an extraordinary purpose, and I hope that at one point or other in the film you might even sympathize with the reasons that he's doing what he's doing, not necessarily the means and the destruction he causes. But it was a great ride, not just because he's the bad guy and the antagonist but also because he has a purpose and it's hard not to see his point of view at certain points." But of course, Benedict was playing Khan. All he was doing was helping to keep the true identity of his character under wraps.

After the film was released and the secret was out though, Benedict admitted he wasn't sure if it had been a good or bad idea to hide his character's identity. It was, after all, Abrams's decision not to let the cat out of the bag before release day. "I was fine with it. The intention was to have the reveal for the audience that was going to be thrilling, people were going to go, [gasps] 'Really!?' And that worked to an extent, because not everyone knew what they were in for when they went into the theatre and some people wanted to join in that thrill of seeing it and experiencing it in the theatre rather than having it spoiled from reviews or Internet gossip or trailers that gave everything away. So, who knows? For those people, I would say it was a good thing. For anyone else who wants to find out, you know, there are always ways of finding out. And people have their hunches. But I sat in a couple of theatres ... and both times, it was like, 'Yeah! Whoa!' There was a verbal and physical reaction to it. So I was like, well, there, it kind of works." And he was right.

Despite the secrecy over the plot and characters, there wasn't quite the same mystery over some of the key locations that were being used during production. One of the most impressive moments for Benedict was shooting some scenes in the now iconic Budweiser Brewery in the San Fernando Valley, which was utilized as the engine room of the Starship *Enterprise* in Abrams's previous *Star Trek* outing. "It's noisy!" was Benedict's memory of the place. "It's very, very, very, mind-numbingly noisy. It's slightly like what you would imagine they would be playing in your earphones if you were being tortured by some foreign operative. It's not particularly pleasant and yet it's stunning and it films beautifully. It's incredible. It's a working, functioning factory and production doesn't shut down for us being there. It's fantastic, really beautiful."

Ten years before, Benedict could never have imagined himself gushing on about the inside of a beer factory. But then again, ten years previously, when he had been playing Shakespeare in a London park or taking parts on long-forgotten TV shows, he would never have imagined himself as the latest Brit to play a big Hollywood baddie. And the *Star Trek* role was the biggest he could have hoped for.

As soon as filming began, it was mayhem. Fans managed to send autograph requests to Benedict via Paramount Studios. In the US, Benedict was only known for his role as Sherlock at this time, and he certainly wasn't yet what the film industry likes to describe as a "hot property." But within a few weeks of it becoming common knowledge that he was on board the new *Star Trek* movie, not only did Trekkers/Trekkies clamour for any insider information and leaked photographs showing Benedict in a deadly battle with Zachary Quinto's Spock, but Benedict fans also scoured websites and studio locations for a glimpse of the latest *Star Trek* villain. After a now famous photo leak, Abrams had a huge wall constructed around the set to prevent paparazzi or over-zealous fans from getting too close a look at filming.

One year after the film had wrapped, the cinema-going public would enjoy the first glimpse of Benedict's stellar performance as the latest big-screen baddie when Paramount released a teaser trailer into cinemas for Christmas 2012. Fans were given some clues of what to expect from the new *Star Trek*, "coming soon to a multiplex near you!" Carefully timed to coincide with a peak movie-going time of the year, a nine-minute trailer was also distributed into selected IMAX theatres in the US at the same times that *The Hobbit* was showing, providing a welcome cross-promotion opportunity for Benedict. Two months later, magazines such as *Empire* and *Entertainment Weekly* both featured Benedict in his *Star Trek* role on the covers of their February 2013 issues, just three months ahead of the film's May 2013 premiere. In the UK, the film would be released one week before American audiences would be able to see it, indicating not only intense interest in what was expected to become the summer blockbuster, but also giving Benedict's home turf an advantage.

Benedict, the boy from Hammersmith, was right there in the thick of it. He was the insider who would unleash hell on the future. The transformation from goodie to baddie had worked a treat. Now he was not just the star of the most popular detective series on television, he was also the sci-fi villain of the year's biggest blockbuster. His only concern was the Trekkies, the super fans who guard every aspect of the franchise. How would they react? Benedict hoped he was ready for this, but Hollywood advisers always suggest a strategy of self-preservation – which means avoiding as much Internet comment as possible. He took the advice on board, saying he knew it would paralyze him if he read all the comments. But if the fans were happy, "I'll be over the moon."

Whether you loved it or not, there was no denying that *Star Trek Into Darkness* was a breathtaking achievement, and with Paramount's nominations to the Academy Award voters that the film be considered for Best Picture and Benedict for Best Supporting Actor at the 2014 Oscars, it couldn't get much better.

Chapter 10

Back to Basics

The first indication that the US had a severe case of Benaddiction came in New York in May 2012 at a preview screening of the latest *Sherlock* series. It had had been set up in a modest theatre in midtown Manhattan. "The theatre had 400 seats but more than 10,000 applied to get in, and dozens stood in line for 12 hours to be assured of a good seat," recalls Sue Vertue. The atmosphere was amazing and it kept getting better. When Benedict took to the stage for a Q&A session, the organizers said the cheers from the crowd were worthy of a Justin Bieber concert. "The atmosphere in the room was electric, it was great for Benedict."

The show was broadcast on Sunday nights and got double the average primetime PBS audience. It also topped the US iTunes television download chart and got some blue-chip awards. "Sherlock: He's sexy and he knows it," shouted the *Washington Post*, renowned for not being enthusiastic about primetime TV in general. The *Hollywood Reporter*, however, gave it an even better review. American journalists said they flocked to Benedict's side because he was always happy to talk, and he was always guaranteed to speak his mind. LA-based celebrity blogger Danny Deloitte said Benedict brought two vital elements to an interview: intelligence and excitement. "He's not been media-trained to within an inch of his life. He's not like a classic Hollywood wannabe who's so desperate not to offend his next casting agent that he won't dare express any opinions. Neither is he so dumb that he doesn't have any opinions. He's educated and he's got plenty of life experience. That's a breath of fresh air for people like me."

Known to the press as unguarded and cheerfully forthcoming, Benedict himself admits that he doesn't police himself very much in interviews. Many journalists say it's clear that "he thinks, he explains, he goes off on tangents, he thinks again, explains again," and along the way, he gives good copy. None better, perhaps, than when he apparently criticized *Downton Abbey* a few weeks before his then latest drama *Parade's End* was about to be screened. What looked like a bid to win viewers for one drama over the other somehow seems to have been blown out of all proportion. Despite being good friends with the *Downton Abbey* creator Julian Fellowes as well as several of the cast, the Internet was alive with the story that he had called the show "sentimental, clichéd and fucking atrocious." But did he really? Not according to Fellowes. He was not at all riled by the comments that appeared in almost every newspaper in the land. "I have known Ben since he was a little boy and I couldn't be fonder of him. He has turned out to be a marvellous actor and I will certainly watch *Parade's End*, which has a wonderful cast and, in Tom Stoppard, a brilliant writer. I am quite sure what Ben said has been taken out of context and does not at all reflect Ben's real feelings. The popularity of *Downton* and Ben's series *Sherlock*, and, hopefully, *Parade's End* are all part of a surge of interest in television drama which can only be good news for all of us."

There were others, however, who loved the story. "It allowed us to write about the hottest new actor and the hottest old show in town," says Deloitte. But for all the international furore his comments caused, Benedict swears it was all a giant mistake. "Suddenly I'm in the middle of a PR disaster. Maybe I am a PR disaster because I talk too much or don't filter enough. But I was kind of mortified," he said when the fuss finally died down.

Not that he was alone, there were many who could sympathize with him about the tabloid press picking up the wrong end of the stick and taking the comments from a *Reader's Digest* interview literally. Nor did Benedict have the time to worry about it too much. Far from the tabloid press, and well under the radar of public scrutiny, he was busy at work on another two major film projects.

The first was the real-life drama *12 Years a Slave*. Ever since it premiered at the Toronto Film Festival in September 2013, the movie has received nothing but praise. The *New Yorker's* critic David Denby described it as "easily the greatest feature film ever made about American slavery" when it was released nationally in the US one month after Toronto. However, for other reviewers, it wasn't quite the definitive depiction of slavery, nor the first. Aside from

Spielberg's *Amistad*, Tarantino's *Django Unchained*, and Benedict's own *Amazing Grace*, many are still moved by Alex Haley's *Roots* for its reality and heart in its telling of how Haley's family moved from slavery to liberation. But most agreed, there is a lot to like about *12 Years a Slave*. The film was adapted from the 1853 memoir by Solomon Northup, who had been a free black man in upstate New York. A husband and father, he was a literate, working man, who also made money as a fiddler. But in 1841, after being lured to Washington, DC with the promise of several days' work playing with the circus, he was kidnapped into slavery. Over the next 12 years, he became the property of a series of different plantation owners – one of whom was especially cruel and brutal.

The book *Twelve Years a Slave* vividly recounts the terrible suffering Northup endured at the hands of several slave owners before being rescued in 1853. Published that same year, it was a bestseller and it seems incredible that it took another 160 years for it to be made into a film. It all came about when British film director Steve McQueen decided to explore American slavery in a way that hadn't been done so on screen before – from the point of view of a man who had known both the joy of freedom and the injustice of human bondage. He was aware that, historically, some Southern slaves had been kidnapped from Northern states, but only later would he learn that a memoir of the precise experience he was now imagining already existed.

"Certainly," explains McQueen, "I wanted to tell a story about slavery, and it was just one of those subject matters where I thought to myself, 'how do I approach this?' I liked the idea of it starting

Right: Mark Gatiss, Benedict and Martin Freeman share the glory of their *Sherlock* awards at the British Academy Television Awards in London, May 2011.

Below: Playing creator and creature in Danny Boyle's *Frankenstein* at The Royal Court in February 2011 was one of the most challenging and exhausting stage roles that Benedict took on. He is shown here with Jonny Lee Miller, whom he alternated roles with on alternate performances.

Above: Sharing a tense moment with Patrick Kennedy and Tom Hiddleston in Steven Speilberg's *War Horse*.

Left: Benedict with Steven Spielberg during the London premiere of *War Horse* at the Odeon Leicester Square in January 2012.

Above: Playing a British spy in *Tinker Tailor Soldier Spy* was a role Benedict had always wanted to play. He called it the ultimate acting experience. He is pictured here with co-star Gary Oldman.

Right: Benedict signing autographs for fans at the stage door of the Duke of York's Theatre in London before a rehearsal reading for *Look Back in Anger*.

From Baker Street to deep space. Benedict as sci-fi baddie John Harrison in *Star Trek Into Darkness*, J.J Abrams second outing with the crew of the Enterprise.

Above: Benedict with Chiwetel Ejiofor in a scene from the multi-award nominated *12 Years A Slave*, Steve McQueen's film about American slavery that had most critics applauding ever since it premiered at the Toronto International Film Festival in September 2013.

Opposite: Although many actors would probably have turned down the role of playing such a controversial figure as Julian Assange in *The Fifth Estate*, Benedict jumped at the chance.

Benedict as computer pioneer and codebreaker Alan Turing, during the latter stages of filming *The Imitation Game* in London, November 2013.

with someone who is a free man, a man who is much like everyone watching the movie in the cinema, just a regular family guy, who is then dragged into slavery through a kidnapping. I thought of him as someone who could take the audience through the ghastly conveyor belt of slavery's history." At the time, McQueen mentioned the idea to his wife, Bianca, and it was she who found Solomon Northup's memoir, a book that had once shaken American society but was no longer well known. "My wife found the book and as soon as I opened it, I couldn't stop. I was stunned and amazed by this incredible true story. It read like *Pinocchio* or a Brothers' Grimm tale, with a man pulled from life with his family into a dark, twisted tunnel, yet one that has a light at the end of it."

McQueen also discovered that Northup was a careful observer of people, able to convey what slavery actually looked like and felt like from the inside. Shocking as his story was, Northup's tale was also an inspiring journey of both physical and moral courage. With 2013 marking the 160th anniversary of Northup's freedom, McQueen felt his story was especially urgent to tell right now. "This story has far more reach than anything else I've seen or read lately," explains McQueen. "I couldn't believe that I hadn't known about this book. How was it possible? Most Americans I mentioned the book to hadn't heard of it either. For me it is as important to American history as *The Diary of Anne Frank* is to European history, a remarkable account of man's journey into astonishing inhumanity. Everyone thinks they know about this period in American history, but I think a lot of things in this film will surprise people the way they surprised me. I felt it would be an honour and a privilege to turn the book into a film and bring this story to audiences." Known for positioning intensely emotional and sometimes disturbing scenes against frames with a painting-like formal beauty, the story would give McQueen a chance to develop his distinctive visual style, while at the same time displaying his considerable skills as a storyteller.

That storytelling was helped, in the early stages of pre-production, by Brad Pitt and his Plan B productions. "My feeling is that without Brad, this film would not have been made," applauds McQueen. "He made a real contribution as a producer because he is so full-on, direct and supportive to the filmmaker. And as an actor, even in a smaller role, he is able to do more in a few minutes of screen time that most people ever could."

For a lot of directors, casting the role of Northup would have been a real challenge, but not for McQueen. As far as he was concerned, there was only ever one man for the part and that was the actor Chiwetel Ejiofor. Known for a wide range of roles from his breakout as a British immigrant in *Dirty Pretty Things* and a future revolutionary in *Children of Men*, to a drag queen in *Kinky Boots* and a CIA agent in Angelina Jolie's *Salt*, Ejiofor had never carried an epic film on his shoulders in the way he would have to in *12 Years a Slave*. But as soon as the actor's name came up, McQueen was certain he had found the right person. "From the get go, I knew it was Chiwetel. There simply was no other choice," says the director. "He has the nobility to hold the camera and to hold the whole film together. There is so much integrity and decorum to him as a person and an actor, and that's what he brings to Solomon." Even with all his belief in the actor, Ejiofor still surprised McQueen with how truly alive he made Northup seem in the here and now. "Chiwetel went in so deep it was amazing to see," McQueen raves. "It took a lot of courage and a lot of strength."

Nowhere was that better displayed than in the scene where Solomon is left to hang from a lynching noose, his feet barely touching the ground. For hours he struggles just to keep from choking. It became one of Ejiofor's biggest trials in fully entering the role. "The scene is very impactful and really about this incredible resolve that Solomon had to survive," says Ejiofor. "He's teetering on the brink of death but he holds on. It was a real physical strain to re-enact this with the exact detail with which Solomon described it. It was tough emotionally and physically, but there was a feeling for me of stretching back almost 200 years and connecting to Solomon."

When the film was released, Ejiofor was tipped as 2014's hottest contender for the Best Actor Oscar, but he admitted that he wasn't sure he could pull off the role at first. It was only when he got to the scene when he was strung up on a tree that he remembered the gentle humour in Solomon's words from his autobiography – that he would have given anything just to be moved into the shade. That's when Ejiofor realized he could make it work. "It's an extraordinary story," he says. "It sort of drifts away from being this complicated tale of terrible times into a story about the human spirit and I think everybody can connect to it."

Although Benedict's role is much smaller than Ejiofor's, it is still pivotal to the story. He plays Northup's first owner, William Ford, a genteel man who admires Northup's intellect – yet is still a slave owner. Benedict dived into the role in his usual manner, using historical research in order to prepare. "It's been very interesting trying to understand Ford's point of view," he explains. "I discovered that Ford was one of the first to get a land grant in Louisiana. He was regarded by many as being a very bright, God-fearing, good man. He was a preacher, who saw his slaves as children of God, and he tried to conduct himself as someone who had great empathy for the human condition and cared for people."

Yet in his very first scene, Ford shockingly purchases the slave Eliza, thus cruelly separating her from her young daughter. "You see in that moment that no matter how much he preaches and acts with kindness, Ford was still basically supporting the system," continues Benedict. "To separate a woman from her child is utterly reprehensible and no Christian man could truly levy that as being excusable." To Benedict, Ford carries guilt like a heavy stone dragging on his soul, which makes for a complex friendship with Northup, one burdened by open questions of equality. "I think Ford is tortured by his own self-awareness. He completely understands that slavery is antithetical to his Christian morals. In the book, Solomon excuses Ford, saying he was born into this situation and therefore must be forgiven for his actions. Yet, when Ford falls into debt, the ugly truth of slave trading raises its head. I think it breaks his heart to abandon this person he respects to a man he knows is vicious and unprincipled. It tortures his soul, but he still does it."

That tortured quality is what McQueen says Benedict captured in his portrayal of Ford. "There is a battle within Ford between his own morality and his need to adapt to the environment that he is in," says the director. "On the one hand, he has to survive in this environment and on the other he's complicit in it. Benedict brought that duality, that sense of both being caring and being weak." Says Ejiofor, "This was a brilliant piece of casting because Benedict has a quality of charisma, ease and charm, which is what engages Solomon about Ford. Solomon really feels he's not dealing with a monster but with what seems like a decent man – it's a very interesting juxtaposition for Solomon to face in his first years as a slave."

But that isn't the case with Edwin Epps, the role Michael Fassbender plays. A vile drunk, Epps is also a tyrant and rapist whose favourite game is dragging all of his slaves out of bed and making them dance a midnight jig. It is what made the film so powerful and often heartbreaking, as it communicates the true horrors of slave society. Although for many, the film's scenes of brutality could prove hard to stomach, it's the sort of movie that the Academy Award voters love – and rightly so.

With the highly acclaimed notices that Ejiofor earned for his role as Northup, Benedict was, in his own words, "flabbergasted" when Ejiofor presented him with his BAFTA Britannia Award in Los Angeles two months after the film had premiered in Toronto. "It feels odd to accept British Artist of the Year after what you did in *12 Years a Slave*," he told his co-star. In his acceptance speech he told the audience that he was totally overwhelmed and paid tribute to all those who had helped him on his journey. "Not only is my job a privilege, because I love it, I love the inspiring people I get to work with, actors, producers, directors, writers, make-up artists, costume designers, dialect coaches, I really do owe this [award] to all of you, and to my parents. I couldn't have asked for two more extraordinary people, they are both actors, so they know this gig, they know what it is, and yet before all of that, they gave me such love, generosity and wisdom, everything that a child could hope to have and that is where my privilege began, with them, so this is kind of ultimately for them, and it will end up on mum's mantelpiece."

In the end, the film did what was predicted at the 186th Academy Awards ceremony in March 2014, and walked away with the Best Picture Oscar.

12 Years a Slave wasn't the only Oscar hopeful of Benedict's films to be seen at the Toronto Film Festival in September 2013, nor was it his only film to be premiered at the festival. The second of his three films being shown during the opening weekend, amidst red-carpet appearances, parties and press junkets, was *August: Osage County* in which he would be seen playing alongside Meryl Streep, Sam Shepard, Julia Roberts and Juliette Lewis.

Based on Tracy Letts's Pulitzer Prize-winning play, *August: Osage County* is a tale of life, death and familial conflict, but according to most critics who attended the premiere screening, it was a crowd-pleaser and one of the year's must-see films. The story centres on Beverly Weston (played by Sam Shepard) who is an Oklahoma poet battling alcoholism, while his wife Violet (Meryl Streep) is suffereing from cancer and drug dependency. Not long after hiring a live-in caregiver for Violet, Beverly vanishes, prompting the family to unite in a search that ends with a morbid discovery. Mother and daughters (Julia Roberts, Julianne Nicholson and Juliette Lewis) are left to deal with the consequences, which is where the problems really begin as the four women have never exactly got on.

The family drama, produced by a team including George Clooney, had Benedict playing Meryl's sensitive nephew, who in Benedict's own words, "is this adorable, really lost soul who's trying to find a place in a world that cuts him out. He's in love with someone who's very close to him, but it has to remain a secret and it kind of tears him apart. He's constantly belittled by a destructively loving and protective mother because of a secret surrounding who he really is. He's a pretty tragic figure but rather a beautiful soul. And I loved, loved the play, so when I heard they were doing it, I thought, I've got to audition! I'd kill to play that part!" So when Benedict was cast, the actor was more than excited. He was also keen to work with Meryl, saying that it was a wonderful opportunity. But, as he admits, it was difficult to forget that you're working with Meryl Streep. Like so many before him, he was so in awe of the multiple Oscar-winner that he almost froze when he had to play his first scene with her. "I just couldn't act," he confessed. "She really is extraordinary and fantastic. We were all in awe, and we kind of forgot to act in character because we just sat there as an audience. She's astonishing. Working with her was very, very inspiring. I know every actor says that, that works with her, but it's a trip, an absolute trip."

But it almost didn't happen. Although Streep's part in the film led her to earning her eighteenth Oscar nomination, it was a role that the actress turned down when it was first offered to her. "I said numerous times that I didn't want it," recalls Streep. "I didn't want to play this woman who is afflicted by her past and by cancer and by her own worst self. She is detested by her children and quite rightly so. I didn't want to imagine all that, and to have to experience it. But my agent kept saying, 'We have to make this happen.'"

It was only following a conversation with an old friend (who was once an addict) that Streep changed her mind. The pair were talking about their own mothers. "My friend said to me, 'You had a great mother, Meryl. She gave you every opportunity and encouragement. Yet my mother told me that I was nothing and would never amount to anything. You have to do this role for me and for every girl who has a bad mother.' It really hit me when she said that because I knew she was telling the truth. I then called my agent and said, 'All right, I will do it.' But I didn't enjoy it, it was not a fun role." If anything, says Streep, it proved to be both physically and emotionally demanding.

Despite what some critics in Toronto said about the film, that it was a "must-see" movie, not everyone wholeheartedly agreed. According to Tim Robey writing in the *Daily Telegraph*, it was "a vastly enjoyable theatrical banquet, if perhaps not a profound one, and is served up in a bit of a rush here, as if they can't wait to get the next sitting in. But you certainly don't come away feeling hungry."

One of the first things Benedict did when returning home from Toronto was to catch up with the friends that, as he told movie critic Peter Howell, "keep him grounded". He also tried to catch up on some well-deserved sleep and resume a decent diet. Then, he headed to the 100-year-old Foyles bookshop on London's Charing Cross Road and to Daunt Books in Hampstead to catch up on his reading. One of his favourite places to visit is the library at the Garrick Club. "I was at school when I first visited the Garrick; my father took me to the library. In my memory it was enormous, very grand and impressive. Now it appears quite small, which it is. But it still retains an aura. It's an oasis of quiet: a stone's throw from Charing Cross Road and the theatre district on one side, and Covent Garden on the other. You sit in silence, surrounded by volumes full of original playbills for Edmund Kean in *Richard III* or *Othello*. As an actor accustomed to reading photocopied pages roughly bound together into scripts, it is an incredible luxury to read these beautiful editions, printed on heavy paper and in generous type. There is a special thrill in handling a book that might have been held by actors and theatre managers. You are touching the past of the magic world of theatre."

Benedict would also display his lighter side and accepted some of the more frivolous invitations that came his way. His publicist, Karon Maskill, says he's a lot less aloof than his television and film roles might suggest. "He truly has a wicked, wicked sense of humour," she once confirmed. "And he's great fun to be around." He was about to prove exactly what sort of fun Maskill was referring to. In the summer of 2012, he strutted his stuff barefoot on the catwalk at London's Men's Fashion Week. Guests watched him living it up backstage holding his three props, a glass of whiskey, an unlit cigar and a tall blonde model – and a few weeks later, with less frivolity, and in a more serious mood, he agreed to give a poetry reading at the Cheltenham Music Festival.

The organizers were thrilled, and not just because he was one of the biggest names on the bill. "A sense of genuine conviction shone through his performance," said Festival guest Maxine Easton. "He clearly loves words, language and poems. He's educated and enlightening and he's also very charming." The poems Benedict had focused on in Cheltenham were from the time of the First World War. He was back in that era in his next television drama as well and readings during the event further illustrated his comfort with the art associated with such a nation-defining time. In fact, he wanted to participate in the 2012 festival because of his fascination with the era, not only through his involvement with *War Horse* and *Parade's End* but also from school. "I've become a bit obsessed with World War I and the music of the period," he said, "It's something that's really got under my skin. I went to a school with a massive war memorial and was made very aware, very conscious of the sacrifices of generations of men our age, in the First and Second World Wars as well as all the wars since then. The First World War has always fascinated me. I even met the last three survivors... in 2009, and during filming of *Parade's End*, I visited the area that once was the Western Front."

But when the publicity began for *Parade's End*, a reporter from *Shortlist* magazine couldn't help but notice that Benedict was playing another tortured, hyper-intelligent aristocrat. "Ah, but it's a fat one this time!" joked the actor, explaining how he had bulked up for his role. He even went on to joke further about other parts of the production, including the love scene with childhood friend

Rebecca Hall. "We laughed our arses off. There was a lot of wasted film that day," he laughed. But joking apart, there were some solid gold drama moments as well.

The story of how *Parade's End* came about had started several years earlier. Playwright Tom Stoppard had always wanted Benedict to play the lead role of Christopher Tietjens, a government statistician who is unhappily married to an adulterous wife and in love with a spirited suffragette, long before *Sherlock* had turned the actor into the country's hottest star. Benedict joked that he agreed to the part because Stoppard offered him a biscuit as well as a cup of tea. But in reality, he had come close to turning the role down.

Although he had anticipated the jibes from the likes of *Shortlist*, Benedict was very well aware that they touched upon a certain amount of truth. No, he didn't want to be playing another toff in yet another historical drama, but then he read the script and discovered that this "toff" was different. What's more, the drama itself had lot of bite to it. In the end, Benedict jumped at the chance to join the production when filming started, first in England, and then in Belgium. It also proved to be a bit of a family affair. Benedict's father, Tim, was in the cast alongside him, which offered father and son some very special moments in Yorkshire where they filmed a windswept picnic scene on Tim's seventy-second birthday.

The mini-series was a co-production of three companies, but the press most often emphasized the BBC-HBO partnership when the series aired in the UK in autumn 2012, about a year after filming had been completed. At the time the drama was cast, however, Tom Stoppard needed to help convince HBO executives that Benedict would be perfect for the lead. The writer, often described as the greatest living British playwright, visited Benedict on the set of Spielberg's *War Horse*. Although Stoppard could not offer Benedict the role yet, he knew he had found his Christopher Tietjens. Even better, Benedict was wearing a First World War officer's uniform when the two men met.

Interestingly enough, Benedict can still recall the moment when Stoppard arrived unannounced on the West Country set of *War Horse*. "We were between takes on the battlefield, it was raining heavily, and Tom just kept saying to me, 'You're having such a remarkable year, Benedict, such a remarkable year.' Then he would suck on his Silk Cut and stare at the ground. It was very odd. I subsequently found out he couldn't bring himself to look at me properly because I was in First World War clobber, and although I was thin and moustachioed and ginger for that part, he saw in me then the image of Christopher Tietjens. Apparently, he'd been thinking about me playing that role for years, and had even mentioned me when it was first talked about as a project, pre-*Sherlock*, when the backers in America were going, 'Benedict who?'"

The problem was that HBO and the US audience in general were unfamiliar with Benedict's work at that time. Director Susanna White recalled "a famous breakfast at The Ivy in London, when HBO said 'Who is this Benedict Cumberbatch?' And we said, 'Trust us, he's a truly great actor and by the time *Parade's End* has come out, everyone will have heard of him.'" Those words couldn't have been truer. By the time the project was broadcast in the US in

2013, Benedict had become a much more familiar face, not only because of *Sherlock* but also due to the vast amount of speculation surrounding his role in *Star Trek*.

The remaining issues were soon resolved and Stoppard, together with Susanna White, was finally in a position to formally offer the role to Benedict. By then, the BBC's full-throttle *Sherlock Holmes* reboot had made him a star on both sides of the Atlantic, *Frankenstein* had sold out its entire run at the National, and HBO had gone from questioning his involvement in *Parade's End* to more or less insisting upon it. "It was a mark of how crazy and different things have got," laughs Benedict. "Fame is a weird one. You need to distance yourself from it. People see a value in you that you don't see yourself. So when I'm told of my sex-symbol status and all that nonsense, I find it laughable, silly. I mean, look, I'm 36, and I've been looking at this same old mush all my life."

Perhaps it was rather ironic that an actor selecting a variety of international roles, either as part of *The Hobbit* trilogy cast or in *Star Trek*, or as part of a US film focusing on very regional American families in *12 Years a Slave* and *August: Osage County*, would be so clearly identified with Britain in his starring role in what was touted as a high-profile HBO drama. It was a well-made, finely acted drama that showed Benedict could carry a leading role in an extended movie or mini-series marketed to global audiences. When HBO announced the broadcast dates for *Parade's End*, which was set to run from 26 to 28 February 2013, critics questioned whether HBO knew what to do with the mini-series. The cable network's promotion was decidedly more low key than the usual media saturation for, say, something like *Game of Thrones*. HBO ran two episodes of *Parade's End* on Tuesday and Wednesday evenings, with the one-hour conclusion on the Thursday night. Some critics questioned why the mini-series was buried mid-week instead of being the centrepiece of weekend programming. Perhaps they were right. One of the first reviews in *Variety* said that Benedict's "emotionally stunted character and uncomfortable circumstances make this stiffest-of-upper lipped love stories a muddy slog," a sentiment that many other American reviewers agreed with. The reviews seemed to lack the fondness of those Benedict picked up in the UK, where he was nominated for the Broadcasting Press Guilds Award in early February 2013 and went on to win the Best Actor award.

Perhaps the drama was an odd choice for Benedict to take on, especially when you consider the disturbing plot line. Benedict's character is emasculated, cuckolded and in pain. Anyone tuning in hoping to find a cosy period drama would have been in for a big disappointment. Benedict, of course, was central to most of the promotional effort as the first broadcast approached. The papers were full of the latest stories and photographs of him. But some people saw through the smoke screen of celebrity and focused on the job Benedict did on screen. One of them was Egan Ferguson of the *Observer*. "Let's leave aside the man for a moment, what a bloody actor," he wrote.

Ferguson wasn't alone. Good reviews came thick and fast. Everyone lined up to applaud Benedict's return to the small screen, and most critics said the show was "superb, thrilling, compelling and captivating." The early publicity certainly did its job when the first episode of the show earned BBC2 its highest audience figure in seven years. But after that, the rating slumped alarmingly. The series ended with a whimper, not a bang, though it went down well enough with Benedict's long-term fan base. *Parade's End* didn't really do much to send the actor's career in any exciting new direction. Not that it mattered, though. If anything, the relative failure gave Benedict a bit of a respite from tabloid intrusion, and allowed him to get on with his private life.

In the calm before the 2013 storm of *Star Trek Into Darkness, Osage County, 12 Years a Slave* and *The Hobbit: The Desolation of Smaug,* Benedict certainly looked as if he had it all. But behind the scenes, a very different story was starting to unfold. He was feeling that his ambitions were far from fulfilled. One of the things he said he felt unfilled about was his building hunger to direct. He wanted to be able to see a project from inception to fruition. "As an actor you are never there for every heartbeat of it." He also longed for a family of his own and still does to this day. "I've been broody since I was 12, but I can't just get anyone pregnant, it has got to be the right person," he says. Not that he had much time to look for that right person. "Oh well, there's always a way isn't there, and I don't mean the Internet," he laughed. "I mean there are always moments and meetings and chance encounters. But to make meaningful relationships is very hard at the moment. Also, I was in a very, very long relationship all through my 20s and early 30s, so I know about looking for the right one, I guess. And it's tough, it's tough."

For the time being, Benedict was remaining single, or was he? He and Anna Jones had been an item for little more than four months and no one was quite sure how romantically involved they had been. By the time the actor had stopped seeing her in January 2012, there had been little written about their relationship to form any conclusion. In the months after splitting with her, Benedict was soon rumoured to be dating Lydia Hearst, a model and the daughter of newspaper heiress Patty Hearst. Even though close friends admitted the couple appeared to be just good friends, that didn't stop the gossip. Even if they were in a relationship, there was no official announcement to confirm or deny the rumours. Six months after the Hearst gossip, Benedict sparked off another series of rumours when he and Liv Tyler were spotted exiting a cinema after watching a movie together and attending a party. While Tyler's reps had nothing to say on the matter, Benedict's publicist added fuel to the fire by denying the couple were having a relationship with each other.

Much the same happened when Benedict was seen leaving London's Cirque Le Soir nightclub firmly clasping the hand of actress Charlotte Asprey. The two had supposedly just attended a belated celebration for Benedict's thirty-seventh birthday where they were entertained by topless burlesque dancers. Also present were Stephen Fry and fashion designer Mathew Williamson.

The stories didn't stop there. There were also rumours and photographs in circulation that firmly placed the actor with Katia Elizarova, the Russian model who had been making headlines with Benedict ever since they were pictured relaxing together at a hotel poolside in Ibiza. Katia claimed she was getting Benedict to give her intensive acting lessons as she prepared for her stage debut in *Sunstroke*, adapted from Anton Chekhov's *The Lady with the Dog* and Ivan Bunin's *Sunstroke* at the Platform Theatre in King's Cross that August. "I've no theatrical experience, although I have done film," she told one journalist at the BMW i3 Global Reveal party at Old Billingsgate. "They gave me the role because I am so Russian. We have a tendency to traumatize everything and have a reputation for being quite dark. I have just got my script and began rehearsals. Ben has been a great help, but he is very strict. He asks me all about what my character wears, and even how she dresses her daughter. I said, 'Well, in a dress,' and he said, 'No, that isn't good enough, what dress?' So I explained that my character is trying not to draw attention to her daughter because she is planning an affair, but he just said, 'Nevertheless, you ought to know how your character would dress her daughter.'" Katia laughs off claims they are romantically involved. "I know the pictures look intimate but it's all innocent. It looks like we are having a sexy chat, but we were actually discussing what we were going to have off the restaurant menu."

There were such news items romantically linking Benedict to various names. The stories that linked him to his *Sherlock* co-star Lara Pulver from the "Scandal in Belgravia" episode or to his *Star Trek* co-star Alice Eve were just a couple that were nothing more than tittle-tattle gossip. According to Benedict's half-sister Tracy, "One of his regrets is that he hasn't found someone to settle down with. You would have to be a pretty smart cookie to keep up with him. I think that is possibly why he has trouble with girlfriends. He is such a lot like Sherlock, he is quick-thinking like him, but not harsh. He's incredibly well read. In comparison to some, he is quite an intellectual."

In fact, just before flying around the world to promote *Star Trek*, it seemed Benedict would rather spend his time with friends, and his friends' babies and children, even though it reminded him of the gap in his own life. "I'm building a home at the moment and it would be nice to fill that home with love and children," he admitted with open honesty, but he was the first to admit that he wasn't in the right place to play the field or to find his soulmate. The man who said his biggest regret was not being a father by the age of 32, had long since been forced to take a fresh look at the calendar. He had just turned 37 in the summer of 2013 and time was slipping by. "I know you pick up an amazing amount of stamina the minute you become a dad, but I would like to be a young dad," he said wistfully, so he set himself a new deadline. He wanted to be a dad by the time he was 40.

Journalists say it is amazing how the subject of parenthood comes up time and time again in interviews. Women, in particular, find it refreshing how honest the actor is about the subject. Even when Benedict was asked what he considered to be his greatest achievement, surprisingly it wasn't *Sherlock* or one of his latest films or television dramas, but his desire to have children. He has even surprised some of his own friends by admitting he has wanted to be a dad since around the age of 12 – a very young age to be having such broody thoughts. The older he's got, the more his feelings have grown. Of course, everyone wants to know why it's so important to him. Is it because he had effectively been an only child? Is it because he went to boarding school so young? He doesn't know, he just wants to have kids.

But, as we have already touched upon, the problem was all down to where he would meet the woman of his dreams. Where could he meet the mother of his future children? Friends and family kept their eyes peeled for any likely candidates, not that it would be easy to fix him up with a potential Mrs Cumberbatch. Even though he wasn't a fan of blind dates, he was more than willing to show up at the occasional dinner party or go to a friend's book launch or head to the theatre.

In late 2012, Benedict was ready to spring some surprises on the work front. Although it was predicted that he would capitalize on his new film-star resumé and head back to Hollywood, once again, Benedict did something completely unexpected. Instead of taking on a new film, television or theatre project, he decided he would return to one of his other great loves and go back to the world of radio drama.

One of the most appealing aspects to Benedict about radio drama was that he could slip in and out of radio stations with only a few people noticing him. After all, who would pay much attention to a tall, messy-haired man in his late 30s, strolling across the pavement in central London and walking into BBC Broadcasting House? But that was just the way Benedict liked it. Not only that, but he had always talked about the sheer joy of radio. He loved having to conjure up a whole world with just his voice. He loved the intimacy of the experience and the camaraderie among the cast and crew. Most of the time, he turned up at the BBC's fifth-floor studios in jeans, black suede shoes, an opened neck shirt and a suit jacket that was often left on the back of a chair or even folded up on the floor. Radio studios, he vowed, are the perfect sanctuary away from the crazy world outside. But the job itself wasn't without its challenges.

Benedict's first radio job that autumn was to record the Michael Frayn play *Copenhagen*. It tells a complex wartime story in which Benedict's role was that of physicist Warner Heisenberg, a genius who in some ways resembles Stephen Hawking. The script is long and detailed, and with so many pages to turn, the cast worried endlessly about the sound of rustling papers being picked up by the microphone. But while the play tackled some tough themes, the recording process was a lot easier. So too were Benedict's next few gigs. He was back in the regular cast of the radio comedy *Cabin Pressure* and the long-running *Rumpole of the Bailey*. The producers of both shows had never expected to keep Benedict on board after his career took off elsewhere. But Benedict never planned to abandon ship. As far as he was concerned, it wasn't an option. The last thing he wanted to do was to let anyone down.

It was questionable, however, why the actor appeared to be working so hard and so often, and felt the need to return to radio drama when his Smaug was opening a single eye all over the world in the final frames of *The Hobbit*. Why work for what must have been very little when compared to his earnings from film projects? At the time, the official trailers for *Star Trek* were finding their way into cinemas, filming schedules for the third series of *Sherlock* had just been confirmed and Benedict was signing himself up for many other forthcoming projects.

Although the actor would most probably tell you he loved working, he would also probably tell you that the money would come in handy for the periods when he wasn't in such huge demand. It all mattered and most actors would probably do the same, given the chance. As a child, Benedict often watched his parents go through lean periods when work wasn't forthcoming. He knew only too well how quickly actors can go from having it all to having very little. So he wanted to put aside as much money as possible while the going was good. But there were also other reasons. Benedict was only too well aware that some people dismiss him as a privileged child of privileged parents. When you have attended a school like Harrow and have been raised by a theatrical family, you are always going to hear people say you have had it easy. There are always detractors to say you were born with a silver spoon in your mouth and a casting agent's phone number in your cot. Supposedly grittier, working-class actors will always complain that the luvvies have had all the breaks. They didn't have to live the troubled years of so many other movie and television hopefuls, auditioning by day, bussing tables by night and going wild with excitement every time some half-interested person recognized them from a commercial. They'll say people like Benedict got work because of his parents' connections, not because of his talent. But then again, the actor has been turned down for roles, he has lost out to lesser talents, and clearly his fame hasn't exactly been handed to him on a plate or delivered to his door. He has had to work for his success, just like his parents had to in their day.

But if the question is how do you respond to those kinds of accusations, there is no golden rule. In Benedict's case, he decided the one sensible thing to do was work and to carry on as usual. If he wants to leave as deep a professional imprint as possible, it is the best way of proving oneself – that he has paid his dues, that he is a grafter and that he does, in fact, deserve every moment of his success.

"I've done very well in a very bad time for our profession, which is weird. When you start getting jobs and see your mates from drama school, you don't really want to talk about it, because you have this innate sense of guilt that it's not fair that others aren't doing exactly what you're doing. I do have that. The number of people my age, younger now, a whole generation younger, who are fiercely bright, over-educated, under-employed and who are politicized and purposeless really upsets me. It's soul-destroying. So there is a kind of weird guilt about doing well. It's interesting, but only very recently have I found myself able to say, 'I've got some money in the bank account. I am allowed to enjoy this.' But at the beginning, and even now, actually, to be really honest, I'm simply thrilled for getting paid to act."

He refuses to be seen as a one-hit wonder or an overnight sensation, and he is very aware of the old friends and colleagues from drama school who haven't had his breaks and who haven't so far hit his heights. It's not to say they won't, but in showbusiness it is all about timing and luck. He is also more aware than most people think about the problems other people face, whether in showbusiness or not. It is one of the reasons why he still works as an ambassador for The Prince's Trust which aims to put disadvantaged youngsters in jobs, find employment for ex-offenders and support budding entrepreneurs when everyone else has turned them away. It is also why he signed up to appear at places like the Cambridge Science Festival in 2013 to encourage and inspire youngsters to consider rewarding careers, whether that be in acting or in some other profession.

Given Benedict's secure and comfortable position, his next project represented a bold and audacious move for the actor. But would it pay off? Over the years, he has won enough theatrical and television awards to fill a mantelpiece many times over, but there was still one major award that was missing from his collection of accolades. Ever since the Toronto International Film Festival, there had been talk of him being up for an Oscar at the 2014 Academy Awards. Even though Benedict had plenty of promising performances behind him to turn him into an Oscar favourite, nothing was ever written in stone. However, by the end of 2013, he had more chances than most – and with one film in particular – to make it happen and walk away with the elusive prize. Or at least that was the buzz around Hollywood.

Chapter 11

The Man Who Sold the World

It was never expected to be a blockbuster, but then again neither was *The Fifth Estate* expected to be the biggest box-office flop of 2013. Of course, not every film can be a blockbuster, or even a minor success, but in October 2013, the people behind the Julian Assange film were horrified when they learnt the news. According to the financial magazine *Forbes*, *The Fifth Estate* earned $6 million *globally*, despite a relatively thrifty $28 million budget to get it made, and on its opening weekend in the US, the movie took just $1.7 million from 1,769 cinemas across the country, making it the worst opening weekend for any major film released in 2013. Not even the presence of Benedict in the lead role, or the fact that the film was dealing with a currently topical subject, could save it from disaster.

Not that Benedict was entirely surprised. "It was never going to be a popcorn multiplex film, but I'm just thankful that it has positioned me as someone who is capable of doing that kind of role. And whether the film has a big box-office or not, the response to how I have performed as Assange has done me huge favours. It's the first lead role I've had and it's caused this much attention." The parallel of it, he said, was *The Social Network*. "Everyone uses Facebook but not everyone is au fait with WikiLeaks."

Of course, he was right. Moviegoers just weren't that desperate or interested enough to watch a film about Assange and his controversial WikiLeaks website. Neither did it help that the reviews were decidedly mixed, skewing towards the negative end of the spectrum. Director Bill Condon realized he was in trouble on the first weekend. "We were all so excited because it was just in the news recently, but the opposite might be true, that it simply wore out its welcome and that there is something about Assange. I do think there's something about him that does not suggest an evening's entertainment. It's so interesting because when something doesn't live up to expectations then, god, you really start second-guessing if it was this little thing you missed, but when something is as big a rout as this was, where there turned out to be no audience for it in a major way, it's kind of extreme. It really does make you look at the bigger picture."

It had all started a year before when Benedict began talks with DreamWorks about the film that would detail the early days of

WikiLeaks and its founder Assange. By November, Benedict had signed on, and by the end of the following month, the rest of the cast had been assembled. At that time, the film was given a working title of *The Man Who Sold The World*, but then, when it went into production a few weeks later, it had gained the snappier title *The Fifth Estate*. Even though many actors would probably have turned down the role of playing such a controversial figure, for Benedict it was a dream part. Based on the non-fiction memoir by Daniel Domscheit-Berg, on paper the film seemed to have much going for it. After all, the script had been written by the man behind *The West Wing*, the director was the man behind everything from *Chicago* to the final two *Twilight* films, *Breaking Dawn Part 1* and *Part 2* – and even better, it was being bankrolled by Disney's DreamWorks studio.

But perhaps the problem really was down to the film's subject matter. Julian Assange founded WikiLeaks in 2006. The journalistic organization was set up as a non-profit, online site committed to publishing secret and potentially inflammatory information and classified media from anonymous sources. In 2010, WikiLeaks orchestrated the release of the largest cache of secret government files ever to be published, and Assange – seen as both a hero and a villain – became a news story himself.

As the film went into production, Assange and his organization WikiLeaks were at the centre of heated debates over where society should draw the line between openness and security. In 2010, did WikiLeaks strike a winning blow for democracy, allowing ordinary citizens to see the unpalatable truth about governments and corporations? Or were the disclosures reckless in the extreme, placing people and nations in real danger?

These are the questions at the heart of *The Fifth Estate*, the first major feature film to explore the WikiLeaks phenomenon, though the filmmakers do not pretend there can be any final answers at this point. Instead, Bill Condon turns the story of WikiLeaks's emergence into an engrossing political thriller, a drama of friendship and betrayal, and a thought-provoking portrait of our information-obsessed world.

As with any emerging story of invention and change, there are naturally several conflicting versions of WikiLeaks's rise. That is why Condon insisted that *The Fifth Estate* should be regarded as just one take on these contentious events. "This is a subject that almost no two people can agree on," Condon notes. "So, respecting that, we wanted to make a dramatic movie that would spark real conversations about the issues raised by this part of WikiLeaks's history. We didn't set out to make an anti-WikiLeaks movie, or a pro-WikiLeaks movie, but rather, to look at the how and why of some of the extraordinary things WikiLeaks accomplished. We chose to present multiple points of view, to pose a lot of questions, and then leave it up to the audience to come to their own conclusions."

The events, of course, had to be edited to compress them into the 90-minutes running time. Even though the filmmakers brought their own powers of imagination and reasoning to all that is unknown about the mysterious Assange, was it enough to encourage audiences to venture out to their local multiplexes? It seemed it wasn't.

"The film is not a documentary, and not designed to be one," says Condon. "A number of good documentaries on WikiLeaks already exist and there will doubtless be more. We wanted to do something different, to explore some of the bigger issues WikiLeaks provoked in the world while also taking the audience on an emotional journey with a fascinating character of our times. What the film represents is just a slice of the WikiLeaks story, and one interpretation of it. There are certainly going to be other chapters in this story in the future and that's part of what made our film so exciting."

Casting an actor to play a man who is at once idolized and despised was always going to be a challenge. Condon knew he needed an actor with imagination, someone who could come up with an accessible interpretation of a man who remained shrouded in mystery. As the search got underway, it was agreed that the one actor who would best seem to embody the single-minded Assange, for all his mix of geeky cool and complexity, was Benedict. Of course, the actor had come to the fore in playing an impressively broad range of roles, but playing Assange would have to be a performance like no other.

As far as Condon was concerned, "Benedict is an actor we still want to know more about and that was so very appropriate for Julian. There were obvious hints in *Sherlock* of his incredible intelligence. And he has that kind of otherworldly quality that makes him and Assange so fascinating."

Not that Benedict would need any convincing. He was instantly attracted to the material. "The story is about a massive moment we are going through in politics, media and contemporary history," said the actor. "But it is also the story of a friendship going through a shake-up in the middle of it." He certainly knew Assange was a divisive figure, but he also was enamoured with the many aspects of the man, particularly his willingness to lay his ideals on the line, to act when others remained silent.

"It's one thing to have an idea like WikiLeaks, and it is another to carry that kind of idea out with the level of skill and tenacity that Assange has," Benedict added. "I have a great deal of respect for that. He had this idea of maximizing the flow of information to achieve just reforms and no matter how you look at him, that idea will now be a major part of our history going forward." At the same time, he also understood he faced a daunting task. He was acutely aware he would be depicting a man who also inspires anger, and who has personally rankled at almost every representation of him by writers, documentarians and others. "After a brief spell of euphoria, I spiralled into panic about how on earth I was going to do this. There was so much to take on, vocally, physically and just confronting the full import of the story. I did a lot of soul-searching. Reading the source material books was exciting, but at the same time I was aware that Julian himself despises the people who wrote those books, so I went back to other material, including interviews he had given. And then I went through a process of marrying this person I was discovering to the script."

It seemed the more he watched Assange in action, the more he found empathy for him. "I would often be seduced by what he was saying and the image he was projecting. He is striking in the way he takes control of his interviews, refusing to just give good television," observed Benedict. "He has an impassioned integrity and holds his line very firmly." Certainly, he added, that unwavering quality, which can be perceived either as bold commitment or stubborn disregard, became one of the keys to his performance. "There was no excuse for not having a somewhat detailed level of verisimilitude in his body language, so I was keen from the beginning to do that as much as possible and Bill was too, but we didn't want him to be in any way two-dimensional. We didn't shy away from exploring the human elements that Julian might prefer to keep private, because it was also about creating a film character in the most fully rounded way."

As usual, Benedict displayed the intricate level of research he brings to all his roles, impressing everyone on set with his dedication. "He found Julian's emotional core a very relatable core, and created something that is not an imitation of Julian but his own impression of the man," enthused producer Michael Sugar. Equally key to the breadth of Benedict's performance is Julian's relationship with Daniel, which turns from a heady, youthful partnership to a serious war of ideals. "I think in a platonic way, Daniel fell in love with Julian and his ideas," says Benedict. "They became very close at the crucial, formative time of WikiLeaks, and they shared an extraordinary adventure. But it came down to a battle of principles between two very different men."

Although Benedict collaborated closely on Assange's look, donning prosthetic make-up, coloured contact lenses, bleached eyebrows, and the trademark ice-white hair to fully take on the persona, he also did extensive vocal work to capture Assange's very particular manner of speaking. Throughout the complex process, Benedict felt the steadfast support of Condon. "You feel Bill's focus is tailor-made for you. It's not just about him getting his shot, he is really going through your beats. He also had a real concern for the morality and responsibility involved in telling this story. He deeply cares about the real people in the story. So while he worked to create something thrilling and engaging, it was equally important to bring an integrity that honours the subject matter."

In turn, Condon was deeply impressed by Benedict's dedication to the project. That commitment to his role even included establishing a personal e-mail connection with Assange himself and a message from the WikiLeaks founder turned up in Benedict's inbox on the very day before shooting began. However, after months of ignoring Benedict's request to meet, Assange didn't want anything to do with the film, nor to meet with Benedict, and in fact urged him in his 10-page email not to make the film. "It was a very considered, thorough, charming and intelligent account of why he thought it was morally wrong for me to be part of something he thought was going to be damaging in real terms, not just to perceptions, but to the reality of the outcome for himself."

But as Condon explains, "Julian has a very insistent take on these events that in many ways no one else agrees with, but his responses to Benedict were interesting and valuable, and Benedict understood that his job was to morph into Julian and to represent his point of view. He got so into the head of Julian, he brought something beautiful to the performance." He was looking for a way to figure out how to both embody Julian and have perspective on him and had he not struggled so with what was the truth and who Julian is, maybe no one would have got the performance he gives on screen. Like Condon, Benedict ultimately sees *The Fifth Estate* as a story leading into a new era that is just beginning. "WikiLeaks and Assange are an unfinished drama," he observes. "As a storyteller, you can only ever give one version of the events to date, but hopefully this version will motivate people to keep looking deeper into what is really going on around them. In the end, there's no such thing as the objective truth, there's only your personal truth."

Since cutting his links with WikiLeaks and publishing an account of working with Assange, the German technology activist Daniel Domscheit-Berg has also become a controversial figure. His tell-all book, *Inside WikiLeaks: My Time with Julian Assange at the World's Most Dangerous Website*, revealed new information about WikiLeaks's operations and personal details about Assange, though some have questioned Domscheit-Berg's motives. He attempted to establish a competing site OpenLeaks, intended to be more transparent than WikiLeaks and to work more closely with established media, though the organization is not yet fully up and running. But as *The Fifth Estate* begins, Daniel is still a wide-eyed network security specialist, inspired by the ideas that he hopes will change the world.

The filmmakers needed to find an actor who could take Daniel on a journey from idolizing Assange to doubting him, and someone who could play dynamically against Benedict. Those abilities were found in German actor Daniel Brühl, who first came to the attention of US audiences in Quentin Tarantino's *Inglourious Basterds*, and more recently in Ron Howard's *Rush*. "We all loved the idea that Daniel is actually German," raved producer Steve Golin. "Bill really believed in him and supported him for the role even though we knew there would be pressure to find someone more widely known. He just brought so much empathy to the role." Condon agrees. "Daniel is the Everyman of the film, so it was really exciting to be able to find an actor who comes in without a lot of baggage in this country."

Brühl was instantly drawn to the trajectory of Daniel's friendship with Julian. "They go through a very intense journey, because they were nobodies, geeks, computer nerds and then they became famous very, very quickly," he notes. "I think it's an important story to tell because what they did changed our ideas of secrecy and transparency. But the avalanche of information may have been too much for them and the organization was fragile. And, of course, sometimes rapid success and attention changes the way people behave." Once Brühl began his own research into the material, he discovered that there were several interpretations on how the history played out. But that potential for controversy did not deter him. "I felt we would be telling one version of the story, based on particular perspectives of people who were there. I think the film shows the very human flaws in both of these guys. It's natural that friendships will change when you are leading such crazy lives. The ultimate importance of what they did, though, lies in the things they were exposing."

Unlike Benedict, Brühl was able to meet with the man he would be playing, which gave him an advantage. "Daniel has an incredible energy, and when we talked about WikiLeaks he still had a sparkle in his eye and got very hyperactive again. He is still a true activist. When I visited him at home, outside Berlin, he had French antifascists living and working in his barn, because they had nowhere else to go. He really wants to help change things for the better. He was very open and shared his sadness at how one of the most intense relationships in his life had ended. I could tell how much this meant to him, and I hope to have portrayed that in the film." On set, Brühl was greatly aided by Condon. "Bill understood that with actors playing real people we needed individual attention as we each defend our character and their different perspectives," he explains. Brühl especially loved establishing a rapport with Benedict, even if the bond between Julian and Daniel eventually collapses. "Benedict is highly energetic, very powerful, very funny and he has great, spontaneous ideas. We really did become friends and I think you can see that on the screen."

When Benedict started filming *The Fifth Estate* in Iceland halfway through January, he had actually been due to return to the *Sherlock* set to start shooting the third series. However, because the Assange project had moved quickly into development from initial discussions to casting to film, the *Sherlock* producers and the BBC decided to change their own production schedules to accommodate Benedict's change of plans, and the filming of *Sherlock* was delayed.

To put off the makers of two other films that were said to be in production at the same time, DreamWorks decided to release a photo still only days after production had started. It showed Benedict with long white-blond locks, seriously tweezed eyebrows and a differently shaped face, which fan tweets attributed to false teeth. Within a few hours of the photograph's release, it had appeared on news, entertainment and fan sites and generated so much buzz, it was even picked up by CBS News and CNN in the US (which had never featured a Benedict news story before). They ran articles on their websites to accompany the newly released photograph. What was perhaps strange was that these news channels didn't usually promote entertainment stories as exclusive content like the E! Entertainment network does, or their online/print counterpart, *Entertainment Weekly*, but the choice of controversial subject matter – both Assange and WikiLeaks – undoubtedly made the story of a film in production a newsworthy item. It also provided Benedict with wider coverage in the States simply because he was now the star of a forthcoming movie that was already being regarded as a controversial one, and would no doubt be a potential crowd puller – or so it was thought.

Indeed, when DreamWorks finally announced that they would be releasing the film in America in November 2013, most were surprised at how quickly it had been completed and readied for national screening. One of the reasons was probably to ensure that *The Fifth Estate* could be in the running for some Academy Award nominations at the 2014 Oscars, and with Benedict as the film's lead, it was very likely that DreamWorks would put him forward for a Best Actor consideration. If the nomination had been successful, then Benedict's future in Hollywood would have been guaranteed.

In the end, though, when the 2014 Oscar nominations were announced on 16 January, neither film or actor were included, so all the media buzz that Benedict might be an Oscar favourite for his performance seemed nothing more than wishful thinking.

As had been the case with *Star Trek Into Darkness*, the studio was most careful to protect the whereabouts of filming locations. The only information released was that filming was taking place somewhere abroad, away from Benedict's London home base. But that didn't stop fans sharing grainy photos on Twitter and other social media sites of Benedict on set in Iceland. Further debates were triggered when the production shoot moved to Germany. There were even tweets about the casting of extras and the film's current shooting location, once again illustrating how closely fans were following Benedict's movements, and how effectively they established their own network. Unlike the previous year, when a few lucky fans received autographs and replies to mail addressed to him via Paramount, by 2013, the actor and studio were much more secretive and guarded about their production schedules and Benedict's whereabouts, simply because he was now being more methodically sought out by a greater number of fans.

Not that Benedict could escape the gaze of onlookers when he started filming the Alan Turing biopic, *The Imitation Game*, 10 days after *The Fifth Estate* had been given its world premiere at the Toronto Film Festival. On location at King's Cross in London where shooting commenced on 15 September 2013, a small portion of the station had been transformed into the King's Cross of the 1940s for Benedict and his co-star Keira Knightley to shoot their first scenes together. According to Internet sources, *The Imitation Game* – based on a script by Graham Moore – would focus on "the nail-biting race against time by Alan Turing and his brilliant team at Britain's top-secret code-breaking centre, Bletchley Park, during the darkest days of the Second World War." Even before the cameras started rolling, the film was being compared to *Enigma*, the 2001 drama about cryptanalysts at Bletchley Park, starring Dougray Scott and Kate Winslet. According to industry insiders, Moore's screenplay had been purchased for a seven-figure sum by Warner Bros in 2011, with Leonardo DiCaprio in the running to play Turing, but as film buffs have since noted, Benedict was a much better bet. Not only did he have the advantage of actually being English like the real Turing, but he also possesses the sort of scholarly appearance and gentle features that are called for in such a role.

At the end of 2013, when filming had been completed and the first image of Benedict in the role of Turing had been released, the computer pioneer and code-breaker was given a posthumous royal pardon for his 1952 conviction of homosexuality. To many, including former prime minister Gordon Brown, Turing's conviction had been an appalling way for the British establishment to treat someone who had been responsible for cracking the German Enigma code – an achievement that no doubt shortened the length of the Second World War. Quite tragically, two years after Turing was convicted on charges of "gross indecency" and sentenced to chemical castration, he committed suicide at the age of 41.

Just over one week later, on a stormy and bleak New Year's Day in 2014, Benedict was back on the small screen for the third series of *Sherlock* after a two-year absence. The new episodes completely outshone any previous episodes and the series became the most watched non *Doctor Who* drama on British television since 2002. It knocked the ratings for *Call the Midwife* and Hayley's departure from *Coronation Street* for six, with more than nine million people tuning into watch it on the night, and another three million watching it on catch-up TV. No previous episode could match that. It was another four million up from the last series opener "A Scandal in Belgravia". Everyone was thrilled. "When we began *Sherlock*, and it was an instant hit, we thought it couldn't get better," raved producer Sue Vertue. "But each series has outdone the last and this is our biggest rating yet. Trying to believe this is really happening is a job in itself!"

Unsurprisingly, the first episode was the most anticipated episode in the history of the entire programme. It had been two years since Sherlock had apparently leapt to his death in "The Reichenbach Fall" at the end of series two, and then showed up at his own graveside to catch Watson and Mrs Hudson grieving for the man who had changed both their lives. Now, two years on, it seemed everyone in the world wanted to know how he survived the jump. The producers were so keen to keep the secret that pages explaining how he pulled off his vanishing trick were blanked out in some copies of the script to protect any leaks. This is not surprising when you consider that, whilst still in pre-production, "The Empty Hearse" was said to have 13 different possibilities to explain Sherlock's survival, although only three would actually end up in the show. We had TV illusionist Derren Brown putting

Watson under his spell for the few crucial moments that allowed Sherlock's helpers to position Moriarty's body on the pavement in Sherlock's place as Sherlock burst through a window where mortuary registrar Molly Hooper stood waiting, Moriarty and Holmes faking the whole thing in order to get rid of Watson and finally, Mycroft and Shelock's network of homeless individuals faking Sherlock's death to save his friends.

As if that wasn't enough, we also witnessed Sherlock being interrogated in a room in Serbia, getting rescued by brother Mycroft, winging his way back to London to prevent a terrorist attack, being reunited with a livid Watson and meeting Watson's bride-to-be, Mary Morstan, played by Martin Freeman's real-life partner Amanda Abbington. It was, raved most critics, a triumphant return for the most charismatic and fun character on British television.

As Sheryl Garrett pointed out in her January 2014 article in the *Telegraph*, filming the episode was not without its problems. It was a grey, rainy day in April 2013, when Benedict climbed on to the roof of Barts Hospital in London, and jumped off. He had done this before, of course, two years before. Even the red phone box outside the hospital was still covered in tributes, mourning his character's fictitious death. Between takes, Benedict had an umbrella to stop him getting too wet in case it ruined the shot, which resulted in a string of predictable "Sherlock Poppins" headlines when the photo appeared in the tabloids the next day. The constant scrutiny took its toll on Benedict. "It means you can have a lot less fun on location," confirms Benedict. "Before, I might have pretended to swim while I was hanging up there, or played about more between takes, but now you're very aware that you're always being watched."

Normally at a shoot like this, there will be a few bystanders, people who happen to walk by and are curious to see what is going on but, wrote Garrett, "the second day at Barts is gloriously sunny, and as well as the paparazzi, there are about 300 fans making a day of it, standing behind crash barriers and watching avidly." This was despite the fact that, for much of the time, the most interesting thing to see was crew members hosing down pavements so that they would appear to be as wet as they did the day before. According to Garrett, the crowed were "too far back to hear any dialogue, but this still feels like street theatre" and when Darren Brown appeared, there was "an audible intake of breath".

Of course, pictures of all of this appeared almost immediately on social media sites, along with the usual speculation about what their significance was. Sue Vertue had the job of monitoring the fans and asking them not to give anything away. For the most part, says Vertue, "they're terribly charming and polite" and "self-policing". Amongst the fans, there were groups from China, the US and Japan who had timed their visits to London to match the shooting schedule for *Sherlock*.

Once again, the third series was as short and sweet as the first and second with just three episodes.But perhaps that is the secret success of the show, to limit viewers to just three episodes per series. The second of the 90-minute episodes, "The Sign of Three", was quite different to past episodes and took the show off in a completely new direction. Even if it wasn't regarded as the strongest story of the series, it was an ideal opportunity to mix comedy with drama around the centrepiece of John and Mary's wedding and to move away from the usual open and shut case that viewers had come to expect. While this one didn't follow-up on the brief glimpse of new baddie Charles Augustus Magnussen at the end of "The Empty Hearse", viewers were treated to some superb character pieces with the focus clearly on the relationship between Holmes and Watson, setting up what promised to be a grand finale.

While Sherlock doesn't understand the significance of marriage, he is supportive, and determined to be an exemplary best man. There is no plotting to sabotage proceedings despite the fact that a longing glance at Watson's empty chair in their Baker Street flat tells us all we need to know about how he feels. The wedding itself is skipped over entirely and we see no shenanigans, lost rings or unexpected problems which threaten to derail the proceedings. The episode did away with any and all the familiar wedding clichés, although we do get to enjoy a closer look at how Sherlock went about ensuring that nothing went wrong by threatening an ex and bribing a child with pictures of dead bodies!

As Neela Debnath noted in her review in the *Independent* that January, "'The Sign of Three' was packed to the rafters with wit and comedy. There was plenty to leave viewers howling with laughter, mainly thanks to Sherlock's general apathy towards humankind, which despite his revulsion to any sort of sentiment or nostalgia, his best man speech was, at times, quite touching as he revealed just how much John means to him." Certainly, continued, Debnath, "This is the most we have seen the pair express their feelings for one another, usually they are too busy saving the day to let something as trivial as emotion get in the way."

The final episode of the series, "His Last Vow", was seen in the UK on the same weekend that the news had started to be dominated by stories of wretched weather and the misery that was beginning to be inflicted across the country by the torrential downpour of rain and resulting floods. Although it didn't quite pull in the same number of viewers as the first two episodes, it did become the most tweeted about single episode on Twitter, and even if it should have been just what the doctor ordered to cheer the nation up on a wet and windy Sunday evening, many thought the show had lost its way and had strayed too far from its original formula. As some correctly noted, viewers should not have to concentrate too hard to enjoy *Sherlock*.

To others though, "The Last Vow", was in many ways, the best episode of *Sherlock* so far, as it offered a greater insight into Sherlock and Watson than ever before. According to a review in the *Mirror*, if anything, the episode focussed on the relationships between its characters and even introduced us to Sherlock's parents, played by Benedict's real-life mum and dad. "With some amazing visual sequences, a number of clever twists, a truly detestable villain and a strong story, [that led Sherlock into a long conflict with the Napoleon of blackmail, and the one man he truly hates], *Sherlock* continues to show why it is simply one of the greatest TV shows of all time." In one of those twists, after the end credits had finished rolling, viewers were treated to an extraordinary hallucinatory scene in which a video message is being played over again on every TV screen across the country. "Did you miss me?" asks a straight-jacketed Moriarty as if announcing his return from the grave. It was the perfect climatic surprise to end the series with, and an equally perfect reminder, that yes, *Sherlock* would be back.

With or without the promise of a fourth series of *Sherlock*, it was *The Imitation Game* and *The Fifth Estate* that represented the most important and essential steps in the development of Benedict's career. They were a sign of the actor's seriousness and markers of his intent to succeed, no matter what. The boy who was too nervous to audition for a film at school had become one of the most fearless actors of his generation. He had crept through the public consciousness and emerged with a remarkable body of work in theatre, TV and film that would be a credit to someone twice his age. He had defied all those who said he was too posh, too unconventional looking and had too difficult a name to make it big as an actor. In 2013, his biggest fear was that people might get bored with him, and that his hefty workload would mean him popping up on too many screens. He worried that it might look as if he had taken on too many jobs. But in reality, there was little chance of that, not least because every performance he gives is so different.

Today, Benedict Cumberbatch is enjoying a remarkable career. For many, it all started with *Sherlock*, the BBC series that established him as one of the most recognizable British actors of his time and catapulted him into the big league. Although, he had always been admired for playing clever outsider roles in his pre-*Sherlock* days, he was never adored or considered a pin-up, nor was he thought of as a dead cert for global stardom. However, a few years after slipping into the famous Burberry trench coat, all that has changed. Once the rising star of stage, small screen and film, Benedict is no longer waiting in the wings.

Film Roles

2014

The Imitation Game (as Alan Turing)
The Hobbit: There and Back Again (as the voice of Smaug and the Necromancer)

2013

The Fifth Estate (as Julian Assange)
August: Osage County (as Little Charlie)
12 Years a Slave (as William Ford)
Little Favour (as Wallace)
Star Trek Into Darkness (as Khan)
The Hobbit: The Desolation of Smaug (as the voice of Smaug and the Necromancer)

2012

The Hobbit: An Unexpected Journey (as the voice of Smaug and the Necromancer)

2011
Tinker Tailor Soldier Spy (as Peter Guillam)
War Horse (as Major Jamie Stewart)
Wreckers (as David)

2010
The Whistleblower (as Nick Kaufman)
Third Star (as James)
Four Lions (as Negotiator)

2009
Creation (as Joseph Hooker)

2008
Burlesque Fairytales (as Henry Clark)
The Other Boleyn Girl (as William Carey)

2007
Atonement (as Paul Marshall)
Inseparable (film short, as Joe/Charlie)

2006
Amazing Grace (as William Pitt)

Starter for Ten (as Patrick Watts)

TV Roles

2012
Parade's End (mini-series; as Christopher Tietjens)

2010–14
Sherlock (series; as Sherlock Holmes)

2010
Van Gogh: Painted with Words (movie; as Vincent Van Gogh)

2009
Small Island (movie; as Bernard)
The Turning Point (drama; as Guy Burgess)
Agatha Christie's Marple, "Murder is Easy" (movie; as Luke Fitzwilliam)

2008
The Last Enemy (mini-series; as Stephen Ezard)
2007
Stuart: A Life Backwards (movie; as Alexander Masters)

2005

Broken News (series; as Will Parker)
To the Ends of the Earth (mini-series; as Edmund Talbot)
Nathan Barley (series; as Robin)

2004

Hawking (movie; as Stephen Hawking)
Dunkirk (movie documentary; as Lieutenant Jimmy Langley)

2003

Fortysomething (series; as Rory Slippery)
Spooks (series; as Jim North)
Cambridge Spies (mini-series; as Edward Hand)
Heartbeat (series; as Toby Fisher)

2002

Silent Witness (series; as Warren Reid)
Tipping the Velvet (mini-series; as Freddy)
Fields of Gold (movie; as Jeremy)

2000

Heartbeat (series; as Charles)

Theatre Roles

2012
Look Back in Anger (as Jimmy Porter)

2011
Frankenstein (as the Creature/Victor Frankenstein)

2010
The Children's Monologues Gala (as Shephard)
After the Dance (as David Scott-Fowler)

2008
The City (as Chris)

2007
The Arsonists (as Eisenring)
Rhinoceros (as Bérenger)

2006
Period of Adjustment (as George Haverstick)

2005
Hedda Gabler (as George Tesman)

2003
The Lady from the Sea (as Lyngstrand)

2002
Romeo and Juliet (as Benvolio)
As You Like It (as Orlando)
Oh! What a Lovely War! (credit unknown)

2001
Love's Labours Lost (as King of Navarre)
A Midsummer Night's Dream (as Demetrius)

Radio Roles

2013

Neverwhere (BBC Radio 4; as Angel Islington)
Copenhagen (BBC Radio 3; as Werner Heisenberg)

2012

Rumpole and the Explosive Evidence (BBC Radio 4; as Young Rumpole)
Rumpole and the Man of God (BBC Radio 4; as Young Rumpole)
Rumpole and the Gentle Art of Blackmail (BBC Radio 4; as Young Rumpole)
Rumpole and the Expert Witness (BBC Radio 4; as Young Rumpole)

2011

Tom and Viv (BBC Radio 7; as T S Eliot)

2010

Rumpole and the Family Pride (BBC Radio 4; as Young Rumpole)
Rumpole and the Eternal Triangle (BBC Radio 4; as Young Rumpole)

2009

Good Evening (BBC Radio 4; as Dudley Moore)
Rumpole and the Penge Bungalow Murders (BBC Radio 4; as Young Rumpole)

2008–present

Cabin Pressure (BBC Radio 4; as Captain Martin Crieff)

2008

The Pillow Book (BBC Radio 4; as Tadanobu)
The Last Days of Grace (BBC Radio 4, as GF)
At War with Wellington (BBC Radio 4; as the Duke of Wellington)
Chatterton: The Allington Solution (BBC Radio 4; as Thomas Chatterton)
Spellbound (BBC Radio 4; as Dr Murchison)
Doctor Who: Forty-Five (as Howard Carter)

2006

The Possessed (BBC Radio 3; as Nikolai Stavrogin)

2005

The Cocktail Party (BBC Radio 4; as Peter Quilpe)
Seven Women (BBC Radio 4; as Tovey)

2004

The Biggest Secret (BBC Radio 4; as Captain Rob Collins)
The Odyssey (BBC Radio 4; as Telemachus)
The Recruiting Officer (BBC Radio 4; as Worthy)
Kepler (BBC Radio 4; as Johannes Kepler)
The Raj Quartet (BBC Radio 4; as Nigel Rowan)

Nominations and Awards

Film and Television

HOLLYWOOD FILM FESTIVAL
2013
August: Osage County
Nominated for Hollywood Ensemble Award
Won

BAFTA
2013
Britianna Award for British Artist of the Year
Won

BAFTA TV
2012
Sherlock
Nominated for Best Leading Actor

2011
Sherlock
Nominated for Best Leading Actor

2010
Small Island
Nominated for Best Supporting Actor

2005
Hawking
Nominated for Best Actor

BRITISH INDEPENDENT FILM
2011
Tinker Tailor Soldier Spy
Nominated for Best Supporting Actor

BROADCASTING PRESS GUILD
2013
Sherlock
Parade's End
Nominated for Best Actor
Won

2011

Sherlock
Nominated for Best Actor
Won
Van Gogh: Painted With Words
Nominated for Best Actor
Won

PAAFTJ (Pan-American Association of Film and Television Journalists) TELEVISION AWARDS

2012

Sherlock
Nominated for Best Cast in a Mini-series or Movie
Won

SPECSAVERS CRIME THRILLER AWARDS

2012

Sherlock
Nominated for Best Actor
Won

2010

Sherlock
Nominated for Best Actor
Won

CENTRAL OHIO FILM CRITICS ASSOCIATION AWARDS
2012
Tinker Tailor Soldier Spy
Best Ensemble
Shared with Gary Oldman, Mark Strong, John Hurt, Toby Jones, David Dencik, Ciaràn Hinds, Colin Firth, Kathy Burke, Stephen Graham, Simon McBurney, Tom Hardy, Svetlana Khodchenkova, William Haddock
Won

GOLDEN GLOBE
2013
Sherlock
Nominated for Best Performance by an Actor in a Mini-Series or a Motion Picture Made for Television

LONDON CRITICS CIRCLE FILM (ALFS AWARD)
2008
Amazing Grace
Nominated for British Breakthrough – Acting

MONTE CARLO TV FESTIVAL (GOLDEN NYMPH AWARD)
2006
To the Ends of the Earth
Nominated for Best Performance by an Actor in a Mini-Series
Won

2004
Hawking
Nominated for Best Performance by an Actor – Television Films
Won

NATIONAL TELEVISION AWARDS UK
2014
Sherlock
Nominated for Radio Times Award for Best Detective
Won

2013
Sherlock
Nominated for Most Popular Male Drama Performance

2011
Sherlock
Nominated for Most Popular Drama Performance

PRIMETIME EMMY AWARDS
2013
Parade's End
Nominated for Outstanding Lead Actor in a Mini-series or a
Movie

2012
Sherlock
Nominated for Outstanding Lead Actor in a Mini-series or a Movie

SATELITTE AWARDS
2012
Sherlock
Nominated for Best Actor in a Mini-series or a Motion Picture Made for Television
Won

2010
Sherlock
Nominated for Best Actor in a Mini-series or a Motion Picture Made for Television

2008
The Last Enemy
Nominated for Best Actor in a Mini-series or a Motion Picture Made for Television

TV QUICK AWARDS UK
2012
Sherlock
Nominated for Best Actor
Won

2011
Sherlock
Nominated for Best Actor

Theatre

OLIVIER AWARD
2011
Hedda Gabler
Nominated for Best Supporting Actor

2012
Frankenstein
Nominated for Best Actor (with Jonny Lee Miller)
Won

EVENING STANDARD THEATRE AWARD
2011
Frankenstein
Nominated for Best Actor (with Jonny Lee Miller)
Won

CRITICS CIRCLE AWARD
2011
Frankenstein
Nominated for Best Actor
Won

WHAT'S ON STAGE AWARDS
2011
After the Dance
Nominated for Best Actor

2013

Frankenstein

Nominated for Best Actor

IAN CHARLESON AWARDS

2001

Love's Labours Lost

Nominated for Best Classical Stage Performance

2005

Hedda Gabler

Nominated for Best Classical Stage Performance

Won

Film Glossary by Charlotte Rasmussen

The following is a guide to some of the definitions frequently used in the technical and creative side of filmmaking:

Ad lib

From the Latin phrase *ad libitum,* meaning "in accordance with desire", this is improvised dialogue where the actors make up what they say in real time on the movie set or on stage. When in the exact situation required by the script, the actors (or the director) often discover that the production may benefit from a different dialogue or reaction. This way, the final result is often much improved.

Agent

The manager responsible for the professional business dealings of an actor, director, screenwriter or other artist, an agent typically negotiates the contracts and often has some part in selecting or recommending roles for their client. Professional actors usually have assistants, publicists and other personnel in addition to their agent, involved in handling their day-to-day schedule and career.

Billing

The placement (or display) of names of actors, directors and producers for a movie in publicity materials, opening (or closing) film credits and on theatre marquees. A person's status is indicated by the size, relative position and placement of their name. Generally, positions closer to the top, with larger and more prominent letters, designate higher importance and greater box-office draw, and precede people of lesser importance. The most prominent actor is said to have top billing, followed by second billing and so forth.

Blockbuster

A movie that is a huge financial success: $100 million or more. The gross of a movie is, to some extent, a measure of the popularity and talent of its leading actors and can determine whether or not a sequel is economically worthwhile. Often the term gross profit is mentioned in reference to "first dollar gross" and this form of compensation entitles an individual to a percentage of every dollar of gross receipts.

Blocking

The rehearsal used to determine the position and movement of the camera, actors and crew during a particular shot or scene.

Blooper

Funny outtakes and mistakes by cast or crew caught on camera. Bloopers are sometimes included in the end credits of a movie or in the special features section of the final DVD, also known as blooper reels or gag reels. Causes for bloopers are often uncontrollable laughter, props (falling, breaking or failing to work as expected), forgotten lines or sudden incidents such as a bird flying in front of the camera. The term blooper is sometimes also applied to a continuity error, which somehow goes unnoticed (and makes it through) the editing process and is thus released in the final product for viewers to see. However, strictly speaking this is a film error, not a blooper.

Blue screen

Special effects photography in which a subject (an object or a performer) is photographed in front of a uniformly illuminated blue or green screen; during post-production, the coloured screen is optically or electronically eliminated and a new background substituted in its place, allowing images to be combined. Blue is normally used for people (because the human skin has very little blue colour to it) and green for digital shots (the green colour channel retains more detail and requires less light). Other colours may be used depending on what technique is applied. It is often used to achieve the effect of a natural environment, such as a forest, beach, prairie, mountain or other landscape in a shot or sequence, but also to create science-fiction worlds, or environments that are inaccessible during production.

Boom pole

Operated by a person from the sound department, the boom pole is a special piece of equipment. It is made from a length of light aluminium or carbon fibre that allows precise positioning of the microphone, above or below the actors, just out of the camera's frame.

Box office

Measure of the total amount of money paid by moviegoers to see a movie in theatres.

B-Roll

Cutaway shots used to cover the visual part of an interview or narration. They are often made available on the Internet or on DVDs as extra material.

Call back

The follow-up after an audition when the actor is called back for a more personal meeting, maybe to discuss the script or the character. It gives the director and producers a chance to consider whether the actor is appropriate for the role and to check if there is the necessary chemistry between them and other members of the cast.

Call sheet

This details what is being filmed on a particular day, in scene order. It lists the same information as the liner shooting schedule, plus each character name, any extras needed and what time each actor is to be picked up, when they are required to go into make-up/hair and onto set. Crew and special requirements for each scene are also noted.

Cameo

Small part played by a famous actor, who would ordinarily not accept such an insignificant role, for little or sometimes even no money. Often big Hollywood stars choose to appear in independent productions to support and perhaps draw attention to the specific movie (theme, co-star or director).

Camera dolly

The camera can be mounted on top of this little moveable car. During shooting it is often placed on tracks to ensure stability.

Cast

The characters physically present in the play or film. These are the roles for which actors will be needed.

CD

First generation of optical media with a storage capacity of up to 700 MB, mostly used for music, data and images, but some CDs are designed specifically for video (such as VCD or SVCD).

CGI

Computer generated image: a term denoting computers will be used to generate the full imagery.

Character

Any personified entity appearing in a film or a play.

Composite video

The format of analogue television before combined with audio, composed by three signals called Y (luminance), U and V (both carrying colour information).

Credits

The opening credit is an on-screen text that describes the most important people involved in the making of a movie. The end credit is usually a rolling list at the end of the movie, where everybody involved (cast, crew, studio, producers, etc.) is named or thanked.

Cutting room

Location where film rolls or tapes are edited by cutting out the unwanted parts.

Dailies

First positive prints made from the negatives photographed on the previous day. Watching the dailies often determines which scenes need to be re-shot or changed.

Director

In a stage play, the individual responsible for staging (placing in the space or blocking) the actors, sculpting and coordinating their performances, and ensuring they fit with the design elements into a coherent vision of the play. In a musical, there will typically be a separate musical director responsible for the musical elements of the show. In a Dramatists Guild contract, the playwright has approval over the choice of director (and the cast and designers). In film, however, the director carries out the duties of a stage director and has considerably more say over the final product. A casting director plays an important part of pre-production in selecting the cast. This usually involves auditions and if hundreds or thousands of candidates come in to perform, special staff oversee this process.

Distributor

Organization responsible for co-ordinating the distribution of the finished movie to exhibitors, as well as the sale of videos, DVDs, laserdiscs and other media versions of movies.

Dubbing

Dubbing or looping is the process of recording voices to match the exact mouth-movements of the actors on screen. It is often used to replace the original language with another (e.g. Spanish voice track over an American movie). Dubbing or ADR (Additional Dialogue Recording or post-synchronization) is also used to re-record lines by the same actor who originally spoke them – often the case when the original sound on set was interrupted by unwanted or uncontrollable noise such as traffic or is just too unclear. The actors are then called into a sound studio. While watching the film on video they re-perform their line, which is recorded by a sound technician.

DVD

Short for Digital Versatile Disc or Digital Video Disc. Like a CD, a DVD is an optical medium, but has much higher density. There are many types of DVDs (DVD-R, DVD+R, DVD, DVD-RW, DVD+RW) and they are used for video, audio and data storage. Most DVDs used for films are 12cm in diameter and their usual sizes are 4.7 GB (single layer) or 8.5 GB (dual layer) – both types can be double-sided. Dual layer DVDs have a semi-transparent layer on top, through which the red laser shines to reach the layer at the bottom. Switching from one layer to another may cause a noticeable pause in some DVD players. A newer type of high-density disc is the High Definition DVD (HD DVD), able to store three times as much data as the standard DVD format. The Blu-ray disc (BD) offers storage capacity up to 25 GB (single layer). Blu-ray format uses a blue-violet laser (with a shorter wavelength than the typical red laser), enabling a Blu-ray disc to be packed more tightly.

Extras

Individuals appearing where non-specific, non-speaking characters are required, usually in a crowd or in the background. Often relatives of the cast or crew (who may hang around the set) are used.

Feature film

A movie primarily for distribution in theatres, it is at least 60 minutes long or the script at least 90 pages long. As opposed to movies made for TV or produced for video-release only.

Foley

The art of recreating incidental sound effects (such as footsteps) in synchronization with the visual component of a movie.

Frame

Movies are created by taking a rapid sequence of pictures (frames) of action and by displaying these frames at the same rate at which they were recorded, thus creating an illusion of motion. In the US, film equals 24 frames per second (NTSC) and video equals 30 frames per second (NTSC). In Europe, most film equals 25 frames per second (PAL). In France and fractions of Europe, Africa and the former USSR, another standard called SECAM is used.

Franchise

A media franchise (literature, film, videogame, TV programme) is a property involving characters, settings, trademarks, etc. Media franchises tend to cross over from their original media to other forms (i.e. from books to films). Generally a whole series is made in a particular medium, along with merchandise. Some franchises are planned in advance while others happen by accident because of a sudden profitable success.

Freebie

Promotional samples such as tickets, clothing, gadgets, promotional DVDs, books or whatever the production or distributing company chooses to give away free of charge, maybe in limited numbers. Some may be signed by the cast, or are otherwise unique merchandise or bonus material.

Gate

The film gate is an opening in front of the camera where the film is exposed to light. Sometimes the film celluloid can break off, creating debris known as hair, which can create a dark line on the edge of the film frame. Such a hair can only be removed by painting it out digitally in post-production, which is an annoying, time-consuming and costly affair. Several factors influence the frequency of hairs: environment, humidity, camera position, type of film, etc. When the director feels he has got a particular shot, he calls out to the crew to "Check the gate"; a clean shot is replied with "Gate is good". Note: this problem does not exist when shooting digitally.

Grip

A trained lighting and rigging technician.

Hook

A term borrowed from song writing and used to describe a thing (or line) that catches the public's attention and keeps them interested in the flow of a story.

Independent films

Also known as "Indies", these films are financed by a smaller production company independent of a major film studio. Often they produce small, interesting movies on a low budget, which sometimes get no further than recognition at film festivals and/or are released in a limited number of theatres.

Laserdisc

First type of commercial optical disc (LD) with a common size of 30cm in diameter. 18 and 12 cm discs were also published. Analogue video combined with digital audio. Laserdiscs were recorded in three different formats: CAV, CLV and CAA. Mostly caught on in North America and Japan, only to be quickly replaced by the more popular and smaller DVDs when they were introduced.

Liner Shooting Schedule

This details the scene(s) to be shot on each day, including the set, its location (interior or exterior) and the time of day. Also given is the page number of the shooting script where the scene begins, a short synopsis of the scene, and the cast used (represented by a number). Other details may be included, such as the time scheduled for filming to begin.

Location

The physical site where all or part of a film is produced as opposed to the set or soundstage. If the storyline is based on authentic events, it doesn't necessarily mean the exact same location where the action took place in real life but something similar.

Method acting

Sometimes referred to as "the method", it is a style of acting formalized by Russian actor and theatre director Konstantin Stanislavsky. The actor interprets the role by drawing from experiences in his own personal life in direct parallel to the character.

Miniatures

Small landscapes, towns or buildings built in miniature (and usually to scale) to make effects that are impossible to achieve otherwise, either because it is too expensive or too dangerous to do so in reality.

Option

Legal agreement to rent the rights to a script for a specific period of time.

Padding

Material added to clothing or shoes to enhance an actor's physical appearance or to protect a stuntman from unnecessary injuries.

Plot

The order of events in a story: the main plot is called A-plot. Typical plot structure includes (a) Beginning/initial situation; (b) Conflict/problem which has to be achieved/solved; (c) Complications to overcome; (d) Climax; (e) Suspense; (f) Resolution (or not) after the conflict/problem has been solved and (g) Conclusion/end. Simplified, a dramatic structure of a story can be divided into five acts: exposition, rising action, climax (turning point), falling action and resolution (dénouement), meaning unravelling or untying of the plot). This is also known as Freytag's pyramid.

Producer

The person or entity financially responsible for a stage or film production; the chief of a movie production in all matters save the creative efforts of the director, who raises funding, hires key personnel and arranges distribution. An executive producer is not involved in any technical aspects of the filmmaking process, but is still responsible for the overall production (usually handling business and legal issues). The production company is headed up by a producer, director, actor or writer and is to create general entertainment products such as motion pictures, television shows, infomercials, commercials and multimedia.

Production

Pre-production is the stage during the creation of the movie where the producer gets everything ready to shoot: hiring actors through casting, picking directors and the rest of the crew, making costumes, finding locations, editing the script, constructing sets, doing rehearsals, etc. The production is the actual shooting of the movie (also known as principal photography). In post-production (or simply post), extra scenes or alternative versions are shot. This stage also includes the editing and cutting of the movie, creating CGI special effects, adding sound effects and composing the music score and doing the promotion work (press conferences, trailer shows, billboards, etc.) before the premiere.

Prop

A prop is any object held, manipulated or carried by a performer during a theatrical performance, on stage or film. Examples include a stage gun, mock glassware, etc.

Rating

In the US, The Motion Picture Association of America (MPAA) and the National Association of Theatre Owners (NATO) operate a rating system for movies: G (general audience, all ages admitted), PG (parental guidance suggested, some material may not be suitable for children), PG-13 (parents strongly cautioned, some material may be inappropriate for children under 13), R (restricted, under 17, requires accompanying parent or adult guardian) and NC-17 (no one 17 and under will be admitted). The rating for a particular movie is decided by a board of parents. They also define an informational warning for the particular movie, along with the rating (i.e. for strong language, violence, nudity, drug abuse, etc.). In the UK, the British Board of Film Classification (BBFC) classifies films and videos. The rating system differs from the American system: U (suitable for audiences aged 4 years and over, while movies classified Uc are particularly suitable for pre-school children), PG (general viewing, but some scenes may be unsuitable for young children), 12 (no one younger than 12 may rent or buy the movie; movies classified 12A may not be seen by children younger than 12 in the cinema unless accompanied by an adult), 15 (suitable only for 15 years and over; no one younger may buy, rent or see a movie in a cinema), 18 (suitable only for adults; no one younger may buy, rent or see a movie in a cinema). Movies classified R18 mean a special and legally restricted classification – they are to be shown only in specially licensed cinemas and may only be supplied in licensed shops, never by mail order.

Red carpet

A red carpet is a strip of carpet in the colour red, laid out in front of a building to welcome VIPs such as dignitaries and celebrities to formal events such as premieres, special screenings, press conferences, etc.

Region encoding

To avoid the latest movie released in the United States on DVD from being played in other parts of the world before they have even premiered in theatres there, a DVD region locking system is used to control which type of DVDs can be played on DVD players. DVDs are coded for nine different regions (0–8) and they require a DVD player of the same region to play the DVD. The Blu-ray movie region codes are different from DVDs and there are currently three: A/1, B/2, C/3.

Rehearsal

Preparatory event in music and theatre, this is a form of practice to ensure professionalism and to eliminate mistakes by working on details without performing in public or on camera. At a dress rehearsal the ensemble tries out their wardrobe for the first time and the different outfits and costumes are fitted to match their exact size.

Re-shoot

When it is clear that some scenes don't fit each other very well or the story doesn't come together as intended, it is sometimes necessary to shoot a scene again after principal photography has ended. It may be months after the final wrap when the actors are called back to re-shoot their part.

Scene

Continuous block of storytelling, set in a single location or following a particular character.

Score

Any printed version of a musical arrangement for opera, film or other musical work in notational form. It may include lyrics or supplemental text.

Screening

The showing of a film for test audiences and/or people involved in the making of the movie; often several different cuts of a movie are produced in the process. This is why a DVD sometimes refers to the term "director's cut" whereas the final version that hits the theatres is a collaboration between the director, editors, producers and the studio executives.

Script

Blueprint or roadmap outlining a movie story through visual descriptions, actions of characters and their dialogue, a lined script is a copy of the shooting script prepared by the script supervisor during production to indicate (via notations and vertical lines drawn directly onto the script pages) exactly what coverage has been shot. The production script is the script prepared and ready to be put into production. A shooting script has changes known as revised pages made to the production script after the initial circulation. These pages are different in colour and incorporated into the shooting script without displacing or rearranging the original, unrevised pages. A method of script submission in which the writer sends the script (without prior contact) to the theatre or production company is called an unsolicited script.

Sequel

A second creative work (book, movie or play) set in the same universe as the first, but later in time. It often employs elements such as characters, settings or plots as in the original story. It is the opposite of prequel (set before the original story). Prequels suffer the disadvantage of the audience knowing what the outcome will be.

Set

The physical elements constructed or arranged to create a sense of place. Usually there is a set designer/art director, as well as other professional designers whose job it is to envision any of the following elements: costumes, sets, lights, sounds or properties.

Sitcom

Also known as a situation comedy. In the US, it is normally a 30-minute comedic television show revolving around funny situations for the main characters.

Soundstage

Large studio area where elaborate sets may be constructed and usually a sound-proof, hangar-like building.

Spoiler

A summary or description relating plot elements not revealed early in the narrative itself. Moreover, because enjoyment of a narrative sometimes depends upon the dramatic tension and suspense, this early revelation of plot elements can "spoil" the enjoyment otherwise experienced. The term spoiler is often associated with special Internet sites and in newsgroup postings. Usually, the spoiler information is preceded by a warning.

Stills

Static photographs taken from a movie and usually used for advertising purposes.

Storyboard

An organized set of graphics used to illustrate and visualize the sequence of filming. It looks like a comic and is used early in the filming process to experiment and move scenes around. Younger movie-makers often prefer computerized animations.

Stunts

Trained and professional stunt personnel used in dangerous situations to avoid exposing the cast to any risk or for acts requiring special skills (for instance, diving, falling or a car crash). The stunt is carried out by the actor's stunt double, which is not to be confused with a body/photo double (a look-alike used for scenes where the actor isn't required, i.e. shots where the face isn't visible or for scenes involving nudity).

Subtitles

Also known as Closed Captions (CC). "Closed" meaning they are only visible when activated (i.e. extra features on a DVD) as opposed to "open" captioning, where all viewers see the captions all the time (i.e. TV programmes). They are used in the following ways: (i) explanatory when foreign languages are used in a movie; (ii) for the hearing impaired; and (iii) as general translation for viewers not speaking the language in question.

Syndication

In television, individual stations may buy programmes outside of the network system.

Table-read

When the writer (or writing team) is finished with the script, it's time for the table-read. During this process the entire cast of actors, all the writers, producers and anyone else who is interested, gets together and acts out the script. This is very important because it lets the writers finally hear how their words sound spoken out loud. They pay close attention to the audience's reaction and take notes on what works and what doesn't – for example, do people get the jokes and laugh at the right places? Afterwards, the writers (and sometimes producers) discuss the problems and explore ways to improve the script.

Tape marks

Most times the exact spot where the actors are supposed to be standing is marked with tape on the floor (off-camera), since it's important for the cameraman and the rest of the cast to know where everyone is positioned.

Teaser/Trailer

A set of scenes used for promotional purposes, appearing on television and in theatres before other films is called a teaser since it is used to "tease" the audience and grab their attention. Like the teaser, the trailer is a short, edited montage of selected scenes to be used as an advertisement for the film, a preview of coming attractions. Running times vary from 15 seconds to three minutes. Not everything in the trailer will necessarily appear in the final film since the trailer is often produced early in the filming process. A trailer is sometimes used as a selling tool to raise funds for a feature film. Originally it was shown at the end of a film (hence the term "trailer"), but people left the theatre before seeing it and so it was moved to the beginning.

Trailer

A mobile home for the actors while filming on location or in a studio, it can be a mid-sized RV (recreational vehicle). The trailers may be elaborately equipped with bedroom, bathroom, small kitchen, etc. since the actors sometimes spend a lot of hours there, preparing their work, having meetings, relaxing, spending time with their family or just hanging out and waiting in-between takes. Some trailers are made into schoolrooms, dressing rooms or hair and make-up trailers, where the cast is fixed up before the shoot. For temporary stays, such as on a movie set, the trailers do not become as personalized as they do for larger productions (such as ongoing television shows where the actors often decorate their home-away-from-home).

Two-shot

Close-up camera shot of two people in the foreground, framed from the chest up, and often in dialogue with each other to indicate relationship information. Likewise three-shot, etc.

VHS

The Video Home System is a recording and playing standard for analogue video-cassette recorders (VCR). The recording medium is magnetic tape. Several variations exist (VHS-C, Super-VHS and others), each again dependent on the type of signal (SECAM, PAL or NTSC).

Voice-over

Also known as VO or off-camera commentary, a speaker narrates the action onscreen.

Wide-angle shot

A shot filmed with a lens that is able to take in a wider field of view (to capture more of the scene's elements or objects) than a regular lens.

Widescreen

Refers to projection systems in which the aspect ratio is wider than the 1.33:1 ratio, which dominated sound film before the 1950s. In the 1950s, many widescreen processes were introduced to combat the growing popularity of television, such as CinemaScope (an anamorphic system), VistaVision (non-anamorphic production technique in which the film is run horizontally through the camera instead of vertically), and Todd-AO and Super Panavision (both used wider-gauge film). It is also known as letterboxing.

Wrap

Term used to define the end of shooting, either for the day or the entire production, and short for Wind Roll And Print. Often associated with the wrap party, where cast, crew, producers, studio executives and other associates get together on the last day of filming to celebrate.

End Notes

Author Research Sources

Chapters 1–11

Film and TV Production Notes

Hawking (Vertigo Films, 2004)

To the Ends of the Earth (PBS, 2004)

Starter For Ten (HBO Films, 2006)

Amazing Grace (Bristol Bay Productions, 2007)

Atonement (Universal Studios, 2007)

The Other Boleyn Girl (Universal/Columbia Pictures, 2008)

Third Star (Independent, 2010)

War Horse (DreamWorks Pictures, 2011)

Tinker Tailor Soldier Spy (StudioCanal, 2011)

The Hobbit (New Line Cinema/MGM/Warner Bros, 2012)

Stuart: A Life Backwards (BBC, 2007)

Star Trek Into Darkness (Paramount Pictures, 2013)

12 Years A Slave (20th Century Fox, 2013)

The Fifth Estate (DreamWorks Pictures, 2103)

Web

Cumberbatchweb (www.benedictcumberbatch.co.uk)

Books

The Benedict Cumberbatch Handbook by Emily Smith (Tebbo, 2012)
Benedict Cumberbatch: Behind the Scenes by Neil Simpson (Endeavour Press, 2013)
Benedict Cumberbatch: In Transition by Lynnette Porter (MX Publishing, 2013)

Video

Unlocking Sherlock: The Making of (BBC/2entertain)
A Study In Pink: Pilot Episode (BBC/2entertain)
Sherlock Uncovered (BBC/2entertain)
Stuart: A Life Backwards Interview (YouTube))

Articles

TV Times: *Timothy, Wanda... and the rose that changed her mind about marriage* by Stewart Knowles, 28 July 1979

Daily Telegraph: *Sexy and electrifying – Hedda Gabler lives* by Charles Spencer, 17 March 2005

What's On Stage: *20 Questions With... Benedict Cumberbatch*, 25 April 2005

Guardian: *After the Dance review* by Michael Billington, 9 June 2010

Scotsman: *Interview: Benedict Cumberbatch, actor*, 20 June 2010

Guardian: *Benedict Cumberbatch on playing Sherlock Holmes* by Amanda Mitchison, 17 July 2010

Daily Mail: *A monster double act for Danny Boyle's Frankenstein* by Baz Bamigboye, 29 October 2010

Guardian: *Frankenstein: Man or monster?* by Maddy Costa, 17 January 2011

Daily Telegraph: *Frankenstein at the National Theatre: Is there a Doctor in the house?* by David Gritten, 23 January 2011

Daily Telegraph: *Danny Boyle's Frankenstein* by Charles Spencer, 23 February 2011

Guardian: *What to say about Danny Boyle's Frankenstein* by Leo Benedictus, 24 February 2011

Guardian: *After the Dance, the awards: Terence Rattigan play wins four Oliviers* by Mark Brown, 13 March 2011

Daily Telegraph: *Sherlock: The Hounds of Baskerville* by Serena Davies, 8 January 2012

Belfast Telegraph: *Cumberbatch late for Spielberg meet*, 11 January 2012

Collider: *Lara Pulver Talks Season Two of Sherlock, Making Her American TV Debut on True Blood and More* by Christina Radish, February 2012

Radio Times: *Danny Boyle: Benedict Cumberbatch is 'one of the leading actors in the world'* by Jack Seale, 9 April 2012

Daily Mirror: Why do women go nuts for me? Benedict Cumberbatch on his weird life as a sex symbol by John Hiscock, 13 June 2012

Gloucestershire Echo: Sherlock star Benedict Cumberbatch to perform in Cheltenham, 22 June 2012

Cheltenham Festivals: Acting stars Benedict Cumberbatch, Miranda Richardson and Amr Waked announced for Cheltenham Music Festival, 22 June 2012

Daily Mirror: Benedict Cumberbatch talks about Sherlock and War Horse, 31 December 2011

Daily Mail: Single again! Benedict Cumberbatch is keen to find love as he splits from girlfriend Anna Jones, 15 January 2012

Now magazine: *Lara Pulver: I chose to shoot Sherlock scene with Benedict Cumberbatch totally naked for 8 hours,* 16 June 2012

London Evening Standard: Lara Pulver: The infamous 111-second scene with Sherlock that made my career go pop by Rosamund Urwin, 15 June 2012

Guardian: Tom Stoppard returns to TV for BBC drama by Vicky Frost, 27 July 2012

Daily Telegraph: Benedict Cumberbatch returns in Parade's End, by Benjamin Secher, 11 August 2012

Daily Telegraph: Benedict Cumberbatch: 'Downton Abbey is sentimental, cliched and atrocious' by Anita Singh, 16 August 2012
Daily Mail: Has Benedict Cumberbatch found love again? Parade's End star gets cosy with Russian model Katia Elizarova by Katie Nicholl, 2 September 2012

Now magazine: *Benedict Cumberbatch: I taught English to Tibetan monks*, 9 February 2013

Daily Mail: *Sherlock Holmes and the mystery of why he's so shy about his illustrious looks* by Alison Boshoff, 29 March 2013

The Mirror: *Benedict Cumberbatch on cheating death: 'I was lost in the wilderness, a gun held to my head'* by Julie McCaffrey, 9 May 2013

New Statesman: *In praise of Benedict Cumberbatch* by Ryan Gilbey, 10 May 2013

The Guardian: *Star Trek Into Darkness: how it was made, by the people who made it* by Alex Godfrey, 11 May 2013

Daily Mail: *Benedict Cumberbatch enjoys a night out with a red-headed woman while Matthew Williamson shows his ghoulish side* by Hannah Flint, 29 July 2013

The Telegraph: *Sherlock star Benedict Cumberbatch gives acting classes to a Russian model* by Tim Walker, 31 July 2013

Daily Mail: Sherlock, his crippling insecurities and the mystery of why Benedict Cumberbatch can't find a wife despite being Britain's latest superstar by Christopher Stevens, 2 August 2013

Daily Mail: Ready for his close-up: Benedict Cumberbatch gets a little touch-up as filming continues on Sherlock, 28 August 2013

Daily Mail: Our secret hideaways: From Felicity Kendal to Benedict Cumberbatch, some of Britain's biggest names, invite you to a private view by Derri Moore, 31 August 2013

Toronto Star: TIFF 2013: Benedict Cumberbatch and the Curious Case of the Auburn Hair by Peter Howell, 14 September 2013

It's Just Movies: Filming begins on The Imitation Game by Eli Colon, September 2013

Hollywood Reporter: The Confessions of Benedict Cumberbatch by Stephen Galloway, 11 September 2013

Guardian: The peculiar charm of Benedict Cumberbatch by Decca Aitkenhead, 14 September 2013

Daily Mail: Benedict Cumberbatch shows off his new slicked back style whilst Keira Knightley wraps up in a padded jacket as they shoot new film The Imitation Game by By Elle Griffiths and Sophia Charalambous, 18 September 2013

Daily Mirror: 12 Years a Slave: True story behind Brit director's movie starring Brad Pitt and Benedict Cumberbatch by Anne Witheridge, 6 October 2013

London Evening Standard: Top girl: Olivia Poulet interview by Nick Curtis, 9 October 2013

Hollywood Reporter: Box Office: Fifth Estate Flops With $1.7 Million by Pamela McClintock 20 October 2013

Hollywood Reporter: WikiLeaks Sabotages 'Fifth Estate' With Its Own Julian Assange Film by Pamela McClintock 20 October 2013

Daily Mail: Cracking the code: Benedict Cumberbatch shoots scenes for WW2 drama The Imitation Game with love interest Keira Knightley at a transformed King's Cross by Jason Chester, 21 October 2013

Daily Express: Keira Knightley and Benedict Cumberbatch go back in time as they film The Imitation Game by Kirsty McCormack, 21 October 2013

Hollywood Reporter: Paramount, Brad Pitt Company Feuding Over 12 Years a Slave by Kim Master, 27 October 2013

Radio Times: Sherlock's Benedict Cumberbatch had a murder mystery case in his own family by Ben Dowell, 28 October 2013

Daily Express: Real murder mystery in Sherlock star Benedict Cumberbatch's past by Elisa Roche, 29 October 2013

Daily Mail: Sherlock Holmes and the mysterious case of his 'killer' ancestor, 29 October 2013

Den of Geek: Clearing up Benedict Cumberbatch's busy schedule by Mark Harrison, 29 October 2013

Radio Times: Benedict Cumberbatch accepts Bafta Britannia Award from 12 Years a Slave co-star Chiwetel Ejiofor by Susanna Lazarus, 10 November 2013

Interview magazine: *Benedict Cumberbatch by Gary Oldman*, November 2013

Independent: Sherlock series 3: Benedict Cumberbatch and Martin Freeman provide teasers for the biggest comeback in British television by Gerard Gilbert, 6 December 2013

Daily Mirror: Benedict Cumberbatch admits he 'understands the nation's obsession with Sherlock series 3' by Carl Greenwood, 8 December 2013

LA Times: Gay British codebreaker Alan Turing given royal pardon by Alicia Banks, 24 December 2013

GQ magazine: *The Many Lives of Benedict Cumberbatch* by Stuart McGurk, January 2014

Empire Online: *20 Sherlock Series 3 Secrets From Mark Gatiss And Steven Moffat* by Ali Plumb, January 2014

Film, TV, Theatre and Radio Roles, Nominations and Awards

IMDb (www.imdb.com)

Aceshowbiz (www.aceshowbiz.com)

Cumberbatchweb (www.benedictcumberbatch.co.uk)